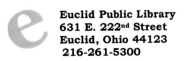

NAZI WOMEN

THE ATTRACTION OF EVIL

NAZI WOMEN

THE ATTRACTION OF EVIL

PAUL ROLAND

ARCTURUS

ARCTURUS

This edition published in 2014 by Arcturus Publishing Limited
26/27 Bickels Yard, 151–153 Bermondsey Street,
London SE1 3HA

ISBN: 978-1-78404-134-2
AD004146UK

Printed in China

Contents

Introduction

The women of Nazi Germany have been portrayed as naïve, adoring acolytes of their messianic Führer, Adolf Hitler, and as victims of a war that turned so tragically against them. They were pitied for the suffering they had endured at the hands of the Soviet army, whose men raped and brutalized them in revenge for the atrocities committed by the SS, and they were grudgingly admired for their stoicism as the *Trümmerfrauen* or 'rubble women' who cleared the destruction brick by brick so that their country could be rebuilt. In stark contrast, sadistic female concentration camp guards like Irma Grese and cruel harpies such as Ilse Koch, 'the Bitch of Buchenwald', were condemned as aberrations who would presumably have become killers even if Hitler hadn't given them the motive, means and opportunity to murder with impunity.

But this simplistic picture is far from the whole truth. While Nazi wives such as Magda Goebbels and Emma Goering lived lives of luxury and privilege, flaunting the latest French fashions in defiance of Hitler's avowed distaste for make-up and haute couture, the wild-eyed women activists who had forsworn such luxuries and devoted themselves to campaigning for the most regressive and authoritarian regime in modern times were horrified to find themselves excluded from the administration they had helped put into power.

Hitler had made no secret of his aversion to permitting women a role in politics and public life, advocating instead that they be confined to the home to fulfil their natural function as mothers of blond, blue-eyed Aryan babies, a role exemplified by the Party slogan *Kinder, Küche und Kirche* ('children, kitchen and church'). They were denied the opportunities afforded by higher education and barred from the professions. And still they voted for him in vast numbers.

However, not all deferred to the dictator. Student activists such as Sophie Scholl and the German wives of Jewish men threatened with deportation protested openly in defiance of the Gestapo, while their fellow citizens remained silent.

But while a comparatively few German women refused to submit to intimidation, others eagerly embraced the opportunities that the National Socialist administration offered them. An army of female secretaries, clerical workers and office assistants dutifully typed up the orders for mass executions, filed details of atrocities and catalogued the mountains of personal possessions stolen from the Nazis' victims, thereby facilitating the process of mass murder. Many of these administrators actively participated in the massacre of civilians, particularly in the conquered countries to the east where the indigenous population were hunted down like animals.

German women, outwardly respectable, devoutly religious and sometimes themselves mothers of young children, thought nothing of killing women and infants with their own hands if the regime had declared them to be enemies of the state. Spurred on by a lethal mixture of ruthless ambition, National Socialist zeal and an eagerness to prove their worthiness to their new rulers, they actively and enthusiastically participated in, and even perpetrated, atrocities while relishing their new-found power. After the war they quietly blended back into German society, living out mundane lives as devoted wives and mothers, never having been required to account for their crimes, or give reasons for their 'missing' years.

Their actions cannot be solely attributable to Hitler's messianic charisma.

CHAPTER ONE

Hitler's Women

Although Hitler was attractive to women, it is unlikely that he ever had a 'normal relationship' . . .

From his formative years as the son of an authoritarian Austrian customs official and an over-indulgent mother, to his violent death in the besieged underground bunker beneath the Reichschancellery in Berlin in April 1945, Adolf Hitler sought unconditional devotion and emotional reassurance from women – yet he restricted the woman's role in the Third Reich to almost medieval status, as embodied in the maxim 'Kinder, Küche und Kirche' ('children, kitchen and church'). Under the Nazis women were excluded from politics and discouraged from pursuing careers, the number of female students in further education was severely restricted and the wages for employed women remained significantly lower than those paid to their male equivalents. Yet still the women of Germany voted for

> HE RESTRICTED THE WOMAN'S ROLE TO ALMOST MEDIEVAL STATUS, AS EMBODIED IN THE MAXIM 'KINDER, KÜCHE UND KIRCHE' ('CHILDREN, KITCHEN AND CHURCH')

Hitler in huge numbers, reaching out to touch him during his stage-managed public appearances like the besotted fans of a glamorous movie star and weeping tears of joy if they were permitted to come into the presence of their beloved Führer.

'The weaker sex'

Hitler encouraged their ardent adoration and demanded they sacrifice their personal ambitions to serve their men, who would restore Germany's honour after the humiliating defeat in the First World War. In Hitler's mind men were made for war and women were 'the weaker sex'. Their sole purpose was to tend the home, serve their husbands and produce blond, blue-eyed Aryan babies to fill the ranks of Germany's invincible military machine. Later, those young women selected for the SS '*Lebensborn*' breeding programme would not even be required to marry their state selected Aryan mates.

Those who were not enticed into motherhood were viewed as either purely decorative specimens for men to flatter and fawn over, like the trophy wives and mistresses of the Nazi leaders, or playthings to be used by any man who desired them. There were only a few women who defied these Nazi stereotypes, one being the filmmaker Leni Riefenstahl, who was fiercely independent but who remained in thrall to Hitler until her death. Another was the test pilot Hanna Reitsch, whom the Führer regarded as an exception, someone who had overcome the disadvantages of her sex to become the archetypal Wagnerian heroine. Hitler's perception of women was that they were physically and intellectually inferior to men because they were impulsive, emotional creatures. The masses, male and female, could be seduced and manipulated by the power of Hitler's oratory because he believed that their collective will was feminine by nature and therefore susceptible to an appeal to their emotions.

Married to the Reich

And yet throughout his turbulent life Hitler apparently refused all opportunities for intimacy, claiming that he was married to the Reich and that he would lose the adoration of his female followers if he got married. Only in the final hours of his life, when he had accepted defeat, did Hitler consent to marry his devoted mistress Eva Braun and allow her to die by his side. But by then he was in failing health and his mental faculties were impaired by a cocktail of drugs prescribed by his physician Dr Morell, whom his aides called 'the Reichsmaster of injections' and 'a quack'. A week before he had told Braun, his dietician Constanze Manziarly and his loyal secretaries Traudl Junge and Gerda Christian that he wished that his generals were as brave as they had been. The women had refused all offers to escape the capital while there was still a chance. But although he demonstrated a condescending respect for women, he refused to entrust them with a significant role in the defence of the Reich.

Hitler's refusal to permit the deployment of women into the munitions factories and other essential services after 1943 proved fatal, by undermining Germany's ability to halt the Russian offensive, while his promise to honour the mothers and daughters of the nation for their part in Germany's regeneration ended in betrayal and the destruction of both the family and the Fatherland.

It is arguable that Hitler's ambivalent attitude towards women originated with his emotional dependency on his over-indulgent mother, which subsequently prevented him from experiencing a normal physical or romantic relationship with a woman.

Doting mother

Klara Pölzl was a simple, modest girl of Austrian peasant stock and was just 24 when she married her 47-year-old, twice widowed husband Alois, a customs official to whom she was related by blood. He might have been her cousin or her uncle. Their exact relationship is uncertain because he was illegitimate, but officially Klara was the daughter of his cousin and as such she called him 'uncle'. She became pregnant with their first child while serving as a housemaid to Alois and his second wife Franziska, who was then dying of tuberculosis. The knowledge that she had carried on an affair while Franziska lay dying preyed on Klara's mind and led her to feel guilty for the rest of her life. When her first child died aged two and a half, followed by its two younger siblings, Klara saw this as divine punishment for her infidelity and became neurotic about hygiene. She would scrub their modest house from morning to night as if exorcizing a curse that had been placed on the family. And so when her fourth child, Adolf, was born on 20 April 1889 she became over-protective, fearing for his safety and believing that if he survived he must be destined for great things and that his achievements would compensate for the loss of his siblings.

Klara became even more neurotic whenever Adolf became sick, which was frequently, and when he finally grew into a sullen but healthy child she, Adolf's younger sister Paula and his stepsister Angela would come between the boy and his strict brutish father, who beat him on an almost daily basis. That is, if the word of Adolf's stepbrother (also named Alois) is to be believed. According to a friend, Henriette von Schirach (the daughter of Hitler's photographer Heinrich Hoffmann), through this intervention 'Hitler must have seen women and girls as guardian angels from an early age' (*Frauen um Hitler*, F. A. Herbig, 1983).

The eminent Harvard psychologist Henry Murray analysed the metaphors in *Mein Kampf* (1925) and concluded that Hitler's aversion to a physical relationship with the opposite sex was due to his 'over identification' with his mother, which 'severely compromised his masculinity' and may have led to him becoming a 'passive homosexual'. It was Murray's opinion that Hitler was both impotent and a 'fully fledged masochist' and that the dictator was driven to over-compensate for his sexual inadequacy through aggression.

Whether that is true or not, it is certain that Klara's almost suffocating affection and her encouragement of her son's fantasies undoubtedly contributed to his narcissistic personality. He became completely self-absorbed and convinced that he was destined to be a great artist, despite his crude drawing skills and poor academic record. His disappointing reports and indolent attitude brought him into ever-increasing conflict with his father, which reached its violent climax when the young Adolf announced that he would not be following Alois into the civil service but would be applying for a place at the Vienna Academy of Fine Arts.

Hitler's only friend

Fortunately for the boy, his father died shortly after, in 1903 when Adolf was 14, leaving him and his mother to enjoy her widow's pension, which was roughly two-thirds of Alois's income plus a lump sum of 650 kronen from his former employer. When the time came for him to leave school two years later the adolescent Adolf prevaricated. He persuaded his mother to allow him to follow his muse, lying in until late morning, reading, writing poetry and attending the theatre and the opera dressed in a silk-lined black frock coat, top hat and white opera gloves, swinging an ivory handled cane like a midget aristocrat. He was accompanied by his only friend, August Kubizek, who had ingratiated himself by being an uncritical admirer and an attentive listener. August knew that what Hitler wanted was an audience more than a friend.

The pair were inseparable, but after Kubizek had graduated with honours from the Vienna Conservatory, his success made Hitler uncomfortable. Adolf's grand plans to become an artist or an architect were exposed as the delusions of a habitual fantasist and even the amenable August tired of his violent mood swings.

'He saw everywhere only obstacles and hostility,'

Kubizek recalled. 'He was always up against something and at odds with the world . . . I never saw him take anything lightly.'

Unrequited love

Hitler's volatile and turbulent nature had manifested itself after he had become infatuated with a pretty young blonde he had seen window shopping in Linz with her mother in the spring of 1905. Her name was Stefanie Jansten. She was 17 and the very image of the pure Aryan girl that Hitler had imagined he would fall in love with.

But he was crippled by shyness and insecurity and only posted one of the many letters and poems he wrote to her. In it he begged her to wait for him until he had graduated from the Vienna Academy, but he deliberately left it unsigned. Stefanie subsequently became engaged and forgot all about her secret admirer. It was a passion that consumed Hitler for almost two years, during which Kubizek witnessed him compose a series of melodramatic odes, visualizing Stefanie riding a white horse across flowering meadows, her long, braided blonde hair caressed by the wind like a Wagnerian heroine. Hitler pestered Kubizek to write reports on her movements whenever he had to leave Linz to visit his mother and he spent long evenings and idle afternoons sketching the Rennaissance-style house he planned to build for her after their marriage. It would have a piano room because he was sure she must possess an extraordinary singing voice to match her beauty.

However, there was more to this unfulfilled obsession than was revealed in Kubizek's official Nazi-endorsed autobiography, as the uncensored manuscript published in English in 2006 suggests.

'Her eyes were very beautiful, bright and expressive,' wrote Kubizek. 'She was exceptionally well dressed and her bearing indicated that she came from a good, well-to-do family.'

From that first day Hitler kept a vigil at the Landstrasse bridge where he had first seen her, with the devoted Kubizek at his side and silently seethed whenever he witnessed the object of his obsession flirting with the army officers and cadets who strolled along the promenade.

It was Kubizek's opinion that the experience of having to suffer silently while these young aristocrats charmed the girl he desired led to Hitler's lifelong hostility towards the officer class, whom he despised for their haughty arrogance and inherited privilege. Their supreme confidence and social status made him feel inferior and acutely aware that his fashionable new clothes would not be enough to impress her. It is revealing that Hitler also assumed that the young officers were effeminate, and in the habit of using perfume and wearing male corsets to give them more manly figures. It suggests he may have suspected himself of harbouring homoerotic feelings and that was also why he did not trust himself to approach Stefanie. He feared he would fail to prove himself a 'real man'. Hitler consoled himself with the notion that Stefanie was only pretending to be interested in these eligible bachelors in order to disguise her true feelings for her shy suitor on the bridge.

> **HAVING TO SUFFER SILENTLY WHILE THESE YOUNG ARISTOCRATS CHARMED THE GIRL HE DESIRED LED TO HITLER'S LIFELONG HOSTILITY TOWARDS THE OFFICER CLASS**

According to Kubizek, Stefanie was totally unaware of his friend's intentions and so rarely acknowledged them when she passed. Occasionally she would offer a polite smile and on those occasions Adolf would be beside himself with joy.

'But when Stefanie, as happened just as often, coldly ignored his gaze, he was crushed and ready to destroy himself and the whole world.'

Thoughts of suicide

The adolescent infatuation soon took a more morbid turn, with Adolf threatening to kidnap the girl and elope with her while his friend distracted her mother. When he realized he couldn't afford to keep his beloved in the manner to which she was accustomed, he contemplated a suicide pact in which they would jump off the bridge hand in hand into the cold, dark waters of the Danube, anticipating the events he would enact with Eva Braun nearly 40 years later.

'Once more, a plan was thought up, in all its details,' Kubizek confided in his autobiography. 'Every single phase of the horrifying tragedy was minutely described.'

Kubizek turns sleuth

To placate him, Kubizek offered to find out all he could; where Stefanie lived, who she lived with and, most important of all, if she had a fondness for one of the young officers. When Kubizek asked why Hitler didn't simply talk to her himself, he was told that 'extraordinary human beings' like Stefanie and himself had no need of conventional forms of communication, but intuitively understood each other – they shared the same feelings and outlook without having to discuss it. When his friend expressed his doubts Hitler flew into a rage. It wasn't the first or the last tirade Kubizek had to suffer during this fantasy affair.

Kubizek discovered that her mother was a widow and they lived in nearby Urfahr. Her brother was a law student studying in Vienna and Stefanie loved to dance. It was the latter which sent Hitler off on another rant. How dare Kubizek suggest that he demean himself by engaging in public displays of dancing? He would never humiliate himself by engaging in such activities.

'Visualize a crowded ballroom and imagine you are deaf,' said Hitler. 'You can't hear the music to which these people are moving, and then take a look at their senseless progress, which leads nowhere. Aren't these people raving mad?' When he and Stefanie were married she wouldn't have the desire to dance.

Kubizek had learned one more fact, which he shared with his volatile friend. Stefanie's real surname was Isak (or Rabatsch according to certain sources) and, though there is no evidence that she was Jewish, Hitler assumed she was. And it didn't make the slightest difference to him at the time. He would find a way round it when the day came for them to announce their engagement. Of course, he never summoned up the courage to speak to her and some years later she married one of those young officers and moved to Vienna.

Had Hitler summoned up the courage to talk to her, the course of history might have been very different.

Fear of intimacy

Hitler's unwillingness to develop a normal romantic relationship with a woman and his pathological aversion to sex suggests a fear of intimacy which could have a number of explanations.

His mother's neurotic obsession with hygiene might have infected her son with a fear of contracting venereal disease, for which there was no known cure at the time. Contracting syphilis invariably led to physical deformity, blindness and insanity. There were incidents of congenital mental disorders in the wider Hitler family which had been caused by generations of inbreeding and the fact that Hitler's parents were blood relations had given their son reason to fear a similar fate. According to the family physician, Dr Bloch, Hitler's younger sister Paula was mentally disabled, his aunt Johanna suffered from schizophrenia and his cousin Edward Schmidt was physically deformed and hampered with a severe speech impediment. Alois's cousin, Josef Veit, had fathered three mentally disabled children, one of whom had been committed to an asylum.

There is also the possibility that Hitler might have been monorchid, if an official Soviet post-mortem report is accurate. (An Independent team of Norwegian and American experts subsequently verified that the remains that had been examined were those of Adolf Hitler.) This physical abnormality can cause aberrant behaviour of the kind exhibited by the adolescent Hitler, namely learning difficulties, lack of concentration, the compulsion to lie, an aversion to criticism, an attraction to physical danger and the belief of being in some way 'special', presumably to compensate for the feelings of social and sexual inadequacy, of not being a 'real' man. According to Christa Schroeder, one of Hitler's secretaries, Professor Kielleutner, an eminent Munich urologist, told Henriette von Schirach that he had attended Hitler in the 1920s and could confirm that he only had one testicle, but that there was nothing he could do to rectify the abnormality as Hitler was then too old to be treated. It was Schroeder's opinion that this condition might have led to Hitler being mocked by a woman, which would have led to his reluctance to engage in normal sexual relations.

Nevertheless, sex held a morbid fascination for Hitler, if Kubizek's account of their forays into the city's red light district is to be believed. One evening, after the pair had been to see Frank Wedekind's scandalous play *Spring Awakening*, with its scenes of rape and homosexuality, Hitler suggested they explore the back streets of Vienna, the 'cesspool of iniquity' where the prostitutes' shameless attempts to entice them to spend a few marks left him incensed and led to yet another lecture on syphilis and the dangers of consorting with such creatures.

Most likely, Hitler's lifelong abhorrence of sex is purely psychological. As a child he had witnessed his father forcing himself on his mother (an incident he described in

Mein Kampf) and thereafter regarded sex as 'dirty' or something only animals indulge in. That long repressed memory, together with the experience of being beaten then comforted, might have generated a sadomasochistic nature which, it has been alleged, characterized his later relationship with his niece Geli Raubal – who was apparently driven to take her own life because of her Uncle Adolf's 'unnatural demands'.

Frustrated genius

But it wasn't only his attitude to women that had been adversely affected by his upbringing. The beatings and verbal abuse he endured from his strict, overbearing father embittered Hitler as a boy, making him seek comfort, safety and affection in the arms of his over-attentive mother, whose mollycoddling nurtured his malignant narcissism. Thereafter Hitler viewed the world as hostile and saw himself as an unrecognized and frustrated genius whose dreams had been thwarted by narrow-minded, unimaginative oafs, who included his father, his school-teachers and the Academy of Fine Arts selection board in Vienna (who had rejected his application). He couldn't accept that their assessment of his ability might have been correct and that his fantasies would not be realized, so he created an excuse for his failure. His teachers were all 'effete', 'abnormal', 'mentally deranged' or 'erudite apes', his father was an alcoholic (there is no evidence to support this) and the academics who had rejected him were all Jewish intellectuals whose privileged background had procured their positions of authority, whereas his poor selfless mother and sisters were virtuous and infallible.

Thereafter he lived in a world of extremes in which an anonymous, invisible cabal conspired to demean him and expose his cherished ambitions as mere delusions of grandeur. His devotion to his mother took on an unnatural intimacy when she became terminally ill. The Jewish doctor who attended her was blamed for failing to save her by her distraught and neurotic son.

Beginnings of anti-Semitism

One of the last times Kubizek saw his friend was when Hitler arrived unexpectedly at the flat they shared in Vienna and found Kubizek with someone he assumed was his girlfriend. She was in fact his pupil, but Kubizek's reassurances did not mollify Hitler, who flew into another tirade in which he derided his friend's efforts to educate a woman.

Hitler never spoke to his friend again. He moved out soon afterwards and drifted aimlessly through the Austrian capital, selling watercolours to the tourists, living on a modest inheritance and bemoaning his fate. Inevitably, in such a frame of mind he came under the influence of extreme nationalists such as Georg Ritter von Schönerer, leader of the German Nationalist Party. Schönerer took the title 'Führer' and espoused a hatred for all foreigners in his virulently anti-Semitic and anti-Catholic pamphlets, which Hitler read with a growing interest.

In a speech to the Vienna Parliament in 1887 Schönerer expressed a common view:

> Our anti-Semitism is not directed against the Jews' religion. It is directed against their racial character-istics . . . everywhere they are in league with the forces of rebellion . . . Therefore every loyal son of his nation must see in anti-Semitism the greatest national progress of this century.

Such inflammatory sentiments were not confined to the lunatic fringe, but were given widespread publicity in the pages of the *Deutsches Volksblatt*, the rabidly anti-Semitic Viennese news-paper, and in a plethora of racist and semi-pornographic literature such as *Ostara*, which featured the ramblings of the *völkisch* 'mystics' Guido von List and Lanz von Liebenfels. Their preposterous and ill-founded theories regarding the antediluvian origins of the Aryan master race were lapped up by the young Hitler. They also addressed his favourite fixations – syphilis and the dangers of women's rights – which he later expounded upon in considerable detail in *Mein Kampf*. *Ostara* was particularly reviled for its lurid stories of virtuous Aryan maidens seduced by malevolent Jews, but it enjoyed a wide circulation among those who wanted to satisfy both their violent sexual fantasies and their anti-Semitic prejudices.

It was in Hitler's nature to blame others for his troubles and Schönerer and his ilk had identified a convenient scapegoat for all of Austria's problems. Anti-Semitism had been endemic in Austrian society for decades, but now Jews seemed to be everywhere – the wealthy ones running the financial institutions and the poor orthodox Hasidim haggling in the streets in their strange attire, looking distinctly alien in their long black coats and traditional ringlets.

> I suddenly encountered an apparition in a black caftan and black sidelocks. 'Is this a Jew?' was my first thought. For, to be sure, they had not looked like that in Linz. I observed the man furtively and cautiously, but the longer I stared at this foreign face, scrutinizing feature for feature, the more my first question assumed a new form. 'Was this a German?' (*Mein Kampf*)

Hitler had finally found a focus for his resentment and a justification for his bigotry. Though it is curious that he himself was often mistaken for a Jew and was teased for looking the part by another youthful acquaintance who he lived with in a hostel for the destitute in Vienna:

Hitler wore a long coat he had been given [. . .] and an increasingly greasy derby hat on the back of his head. His hair was long and tangled and he grew a beard on his chin such as we Christians seldom have, though one is not uncommon on Leopoldstadt or the Jewish ghetto [. . .] Hitler at that time looked very Jewish so that I often joked with him that he must be of Jewish blood. (Reinhold Hanisch, 'I was Hitler's Buddy', *New Republic* magazine, 5 April 1939)

Hitler would not have agreed.

Wherever I went I began to see Jews and the more I saw, the more sharply they became distinguished in my eyes from the rest of humanity . . . I began to hate them . . . I had ceased to be a weak kneed cosmopolitan and became an anti-Semite. (*Mein Kampf*)

One publication that Hitler devoured, *Unadulterated German Words*, even advocated sexual abstinence for young men to preserve their strength in readiness for the coming conflict that would surely test their manhood to the extreme. It also encouraged Austrian youth to stop eating meat because it reputedly stimulated the sex drive. Hitler consequently became a vegetarian and now had a patriotic excuse for shying away from the opposite sex, specifically women of loose morals and prostitutes, who were accused by lunatics like Liebenfels of corrupting and infecting Aryan males with racial and sexual disorders.

> **'WHEREVER I WENT I BEGAN TO SEE JEWS AND THE MORE I SAW, THE MORE THEY BECAME DISTINGUISHED FROM THE REST OF HUMANITY'**

Shaped by war

It began to dawn on the future Führer that fate must have other, greater things in store for him and that was why he had been denied entrance to the Academy. Hitler claimed to have been profoundly moved when war was declared in August 1914. The war would give him a sense of identity, purpose and, perhaps, the chance to prove himself.

> To me those hours came as a deliverance from the distress that had weighed upon me during the days of my youth. I am not ashamed to say that, carried away by the enthusiasm of the moment, I sank down on my knees and thanked heaven out of the fullness of my heart for granting me the good fortune of being permitted to live in such a time. (*Mein Kampf*)

Hitler served as a runner in the 16th Bavarian Reserve Regiment, having refused to enlist in the Austrian army because he claimed it accepted 'mixed races'. And though he distinguished himself sufficiently to be awarded the Iron Cross Second Class in 1914, he was shunned by the rest of his battalion and was never promoted above corporal, because his superiors knew that the men would not obey him.

His comrades called him 'the White Crow' because he never smiled or joked with them and only laughed at others' misfortunes. They found his compulsive cleanliness unnatural and his views on women particularly odd. While they longed to return home to their wives and sweethearts, or bragged of their sexual conquests, Hitler would lecture them on the dangers of interracial intercourse. Consequently he was known as 'the woman hater' and viewed with suspicion for tending his rifle 'with delight, as a woman looks at her jewellery', according to one comrade. 'We all cursed him and found him intolerable,' recalled another.

Hitler returned from the Great War with an Iron Cross First Class for bravery (on the recommendation of his Jewish adjutant, Hugo Gutmann) and a belief that the German army had been stabbed in the back, to use the popular phrase of the time, by spineless politicians and the ageing Kaiser in Berlin.

It was a view shared by the majority of men who had endured five years of privation, slaughter and sacrifice – that Germany had capitulated when there was still a slim chance that its war-weary soldiers might snatch a last victory before the entry of the untested American 'dough boys' could prove decisive. But Hitler's paranoia took a more bizarre form. When the armistice was declared on 11 November 1918 he was suffering from 'hysterical blindness' [Source: Georges-Anquetil, *Hitler conduit le bal*, Paris, 1939] in Pasewalk Hospital, Pomerania after inhaling chlorine gas during the second battle of Ypres a month earlier. There was no physical reason for his blindness, according to his doctor. It was psychosomatic and as such there was nothing they could do for him but send him home.

Hitler becomes leader

The greater part of the German armed forces were de-mobilized in 1919, but Hitler chose to remain in uniform and was sent to Munich, where his superiors assigned him to evaluate an obscure political party that they were considering funding, so that they could influence the political situation in Bavaria.

Imperialist Germany was now a republic. The Kaiser had abdicated and been replaced by a democratically elected president, Friedrich Ebert. But the coalition was weak and there were conflicting factions threatening to destabilize the region. Nationalists like Hitler and many of the men who had returned from the 'war to end all wars' had little faith in the new administration and feared that it would be too weak to stave off the threat posed by communists. Hitler thought the German Workers' Party was 'an absurd little organization', wasting time on points of order and the accounts ('club life of the worst sort') while it had fewer than 60 members, but he saw the opportunity to seize control of the party while it was still small and use it to disseminate his own extreme views.

Within 18 months of joining, Hitler was the leader of the newly named National Socialist Democratic Workers' Party, or Nazi Party as its detractors referred to it, with its own brown-shirted bodyguards, the SA, and an increasingly vocal following numbering some 55,000 members. By November 1923 the Party was impatient for power and gambled on taking it by force. The putsch failed and Hitler was imprisoned after a show trial which gave him nation-wide publicity.

He had been arrested in the home of one of his new female admirers, Frau Helene Hanfstaengl, the American wife of an early supporter, Ernst Hanfstaengl, who later became his foreign press officer before becoming a fierce critic of the Nazis. Shortly before the police arrived Hitler picked up his revolver and, after brandishing it like a ham actor in a bad melodrama, declared his intention to shoot himself.

'This is the end,' he said. 'I will never let those swine take me. I will shoot myself first.' As Hitler had no doubt intended, his little speech had given Helene sufficient time to intervene and snatch the gun from his hand.

'Think of all your loyal followers who believe in you,' she chided him. 'How can you forsake all those good people who share your ideal of saving your country while you take your own life?' Hitler then buried his face in his hands and sobbed while Helene hid the gun in a barrel of flour in the kitchen.

When the authorities came to arrest him he was allegedly found hiding in a wardrobe.

Landsberg prison

Helene's son Egon has said that his mother couldn't take Hitler seriously and felt sorry for him, particularly after the occasion when he fell on one knee and confessed that if she hadn't been married and he didn't have his destiny to fulfil, he would have married her as she was his ideal. When she told her husband of the incident she reassured him that Hitler was no threat to his manhood as he was 'a neuter'. Her husband was of the opinion that, 'What Hitler is looking for in a woman is half-mother and half-sweetheart.'

It was a fair assessment, for a string of matronly admirers visited Hitler in his private furnished rooms in Landsberg prison during the nine months he spent in confinement (1 April–20 December 1924), bringing him home-made cakes and other delicacies. These were the 'Munich Muttis', matronly ladies who saw what they perceived to be loneliness and suffering in his large, piercing blue eyes and desired to mother him. Helene Hanfstaengl's sister-in-law Erna was taken in by this *nebbisch* (helpless) act, but later realized 'these trivialities in clothing and behaviour' were 'calculated for effect'.

It had also fooled the judges, to whom Hitler appeared servile and respectful, earning himself an extremely lenient five year sentence (of which he served less than a year), the freedom to do as he pleased and an entire wing on the second floor which the guards nicknamed 'the general's hill'.

Ernst Hanfstaengl compared the scene to 'a delicatessen. There was fruit and there were flowers, wine and other alcoholic beverages, ham, sausage, cake, boxes of chocolates and much more'.

The prison warden Otto Leybold remembered, 'He was always reasonable, frugal, modest and polite to everyone, especially the officials at the facility' and 'submitted willingly to all restrictions', but he refused to rise before noon or to take exercise. The only activity he had was pacing the room overlooking the river Lech while dictating his manifesto *Mein Kampf* ('My Struggle', originally titled 'Four and a Half Years of Struggle Against Lies, Stupidity and Cowardice') to his personal secretary Rudolf Hess.

> **THE ONLY ACTIVITY HE HAD WAS PACING THE ROOM OVERLOOKING THE RIVER LECH WHILE DICTATING HIS MANIFESTO *MEIN KAMPF***

Hitler's benefactors

The prison records document that Hitler received more than 300 visitors during his incarceration, among whom were General von Ludendorff, the First World War veteran who had been acquitted of his involvement in the failed coup, various Munich politicians and members of Hitler's inner circle such as Nazi 'philosopher' Alfred Rosenberg and Captain Ernst Roehm, leader of the SA.

Listed among the prisoner's many 'benefactors' were several middle-aged women.

Viktoria von Dirksen

Viktoria von Dirksen was a fashionable Berlin hostess, the widow of the man who had built the city's underground system and the stepmother of the German ambassador to Moscow. She and Hitler were close friends in the early years of the movement, although she later became a fearless critic of the Party and disagreed with him over the role of Crown Prince Wilhelm. Viktoria wished to see the Prince installed as monarch, while Hitler was vehemently opposed to a man he considered an 'unprincipled opportunist'. She nevertheless donated a large portion of her late husband's fortune to fund the Party's electoral campaigns.

Elsa Bruckmann

Equally generous was Elsa Bruckmann, the publisher's wife who introduced Hitler to wealthy industrialists and influential members of the aristocracy in her sumptuous Munich salon. In 1926 the Party had seemed on the brink of bankruptcy, impelling Hitler to contemplate taking his own life again. But at the last minute Elsa had intervened. She sent Hitler a note enclosing her wristwatch and invited him to choose any furniture that he might like to furnish his private apartment. When she learned that he had been threatened with eviction for failing to pay the rent and that his Party was in dire financial need, she persuaded her husband Hugo to settle Hitler's personal debts and put their villa at his disposal. She then arranged a four-hour meeting with industrialist Emil Kirdof, who agreed to pay off the Party's creditors and guarantee substantial campaign contributions for the coming year.

Frau Bruckmann was the first of many female admirers who offered their jewellery and other valuables to secure loans for the future Führer. A contemporary record notes that Herr Hitler had deposited, 'an emerald pendant with platinum and diamonds . . . a diamond ring (solitaire) . . . a red silk Spanish cover for a grand piano . . .' The latter was probably a gift from Helena Bechstein, wife of the piano manufacturer, who bought Hitler a new Mercedes for 26,000 marks.

Elsa then bought him clothes and the rhino whip that became his trademark in the 1920s, before he was persuaded that it was not a fitting accessory for an aspiring politician to be seen brandishing in public. The Bruckmanns also brokered the purchase of the Nazi Party headquarters, the Brown House on Brienner Strasse, for 1.5 million marks. This was raised with the aid of wealthy industrialists who were attracted to the Party because they saw in Hitler 'the strong man' the country needed to crush the Bolsheviks and dismantle the unions. In the course of a year the Party acquired the backing of industrial heavyweights Frank Thyssen, the steel baron, Emil Gansser, Werner von Siemens and the board of Daimler, who ensured that Hitler found a sympathetic audience for his speeches in major cities and was no longer confined to the back street beer halls of Bavaria.

Helena Bechstein

Helena Bechstein did more than just buy Hitler a Mercedes. The Bechsteins introduced him to their high society friends in Berlin and Bavaria and invited him to their villa in the Obersalzberg, which made such a favourable impression on their guest that he asked if they could help him buy a property in the area. 'Haus Wachenfeld' would become Hitler's mountain sanctuary, to be renamed 'The Berghof' after extensive renovations and the installation of the famous 'picture window' that ran the entire length of one wall, providing a panoramic view of the mountains. Frau Bechstein later offered her jewellery as surety against a loan of 60,000 Swiss francs when the Party needed additional funds and went so far as to pose as Hitler's mother to visit her imprisoned 'Wolf', the pet name she used while he was in favour and was expected to marry her 'plain-looking' daughter, Lottie. But as soon as Hitler made it clear that he would not be proposing, Frau Bechstein lost her enthusiasm for politics.

Carola Hoffman

Carola Hoffman, the 61-year-old widow of a schoolteacher, had no ulterior motive. She had been an early supporter of the Party and was happy to offer Hitler a home in the quiet suburb of Solln, which he used as an unofficial party headquarters on his release. For a time he regarded her as a substitute for the mother he had lost, addressing postcards to her as *'mein wertvoll kleine Mutter'* ('my precious little mother').

Winifred Wagner

Another avid admirer was Winifred Wagner, the British-born wife of the composer's son, Siegfried, who was dissatisfied with her effete husband's lack of attention and longed to find fulfilment with someone else. She and Hitler met in 1923 and though her initial impression was that he was 'rather common' (he often wore traditional Bavarian lederhosen, which the upper class would have considered only suitable for peasants), she took it upon herself to bring him on. He had every reason to resent being patronized – being taught how to hold his knife and fork, how to choose the right wine and not sweeten it with sugar and how to dress for the occasion instead of wearing a clash of colours to make an impression – but instead she found him a willing pupil. He may have been unsophisticated and poorly educated, but he was astute enough to realize that ingratiating himself with powerful people would be extremely beneficial. Besides, he had a talent for playing the deferential servant, though many found his habitual heel clicking and hand kissing a bit much. She too bought him clothes, but also instructed him in the correct way to behave in polite society, the rules of dinner table etiquette and the value of small talk. The latter was particularly difficult as Hitler demonstrated little respect for other people's opinions and demanded that he alone should dominate the conversation, indulging in long monologues of which he would accept no criticism, only unqualified approval. It was also noted that he was singularly humourless, laughing only at the thought of others' misfortunes.

Winifred's husband's disapproval gave her further reason to persist in her re-education of the awkward and rather coarse working class 'fraud and upstart' (as Siegfried described him) and within a few months it was said that Hitler was seriously contemplating marriage in the belief that the union of their two names would ensure the adulation of the masses. Unaware of Hitler's aversion to romance,

Winifred sent him food parcels while he was in prison and visited him regularly in Munich. After she became a widow in 1930 she made sure she was seen in his company so that the press and the gossipmongers would be kept speculating about when the wedding might be announced. But after his appointment as Chancellor Hitler thought better of it and they remained merely 'good friends'. She called him '*mein Wölfchen*' (my little wolf) and would scold him when she felt he had done something she disapproved of, while he stood shamefaced 'like a naughty schoolboy', according to Ernst Hanfstaengl, and would say nothing.

'He was a frequent visitor at Wahnfried, the Wagner home,' remembered Hanfstaengl, 'and there were many rumours that he would marry Winifred after her husband died. She perhaps came closer to fulfilling his ideal of half-mother and half-sweetheart than any other woman of whom we have any knowledge.'

Sexuality

Ernst Hanfstaengl was also the source of rumours concerning Hitler's relationship with Henriette Hoffmann, the wayward daughter of the Party's official photographer, Heinrich Hoffmann. She subsequently married Baldur von Schirach, leader of the Hitler Youth.

Henny, too, was a blonde and one of very questionable reputation [. . .] Many extraordinary stories have been circulated in Party circles about Hitler's relations with Henny. According to one of the most popular stories, Hitler had once obliged Henny to have very abnormal sexual relations with him. The nature of these relations was not specified, but it was said that later Henny [. . .] had told her father the entire story. Thereupon her father [. . .] had used Henny's story in order to blackmail Hitler.

Whatever this 'abnormal' practice was it could not have been mere rumour as it was referred to by several of Hitler's closest confidants and usually in connection with the apparent suicide of Hitler's niece Geli Raubal, whose mysterious death in 1931 was never satisfactorily explained.

Otto Strasser, whose account must be read with suspicion as he fell out with Hitler and was expelled from the Party in 1930, wrote:

> I knew all about Hitler's abnormality. Like all others in the know, I had heard all about the eccentric practices to which Fraulein Hoffmann was alleged to have lent herself, but I had genuinely believed that the photographer's daughter was a little hysteric who told lies for the sheer fun of it. But Gely, who was completely ignorant of this other affair of her uncle's, confirmed point by point a story scarcely credible to a healthy-minded man. (Otto Strasser, *Hitler and I*, 1940)

Another source, one that must be regarded with equal suspicion, is that published in the lurid exposé *Inside information* (1940) by Hansjürgen Koehler (which is believed to be the pen name of Franz Heinrich Pfeiffer, a former SS officer who fled Germany in 1935 and wrote a series of sensationalist anti-Nazi books). Koehler states:

> As a young girl [Henny] lived with her father in close proximity to Hitler. She was extremely pretty and attractive, and it appears that Hitler was in love with her for a while. But Hitler's make-up [. . .] prevented him from making normal approaches to her. So Henny was very soon disgusted and turned her attentions elsewhere like his earlier flames [. . .] I had occasion to live for some months under the same roof as Hitler, and I have repeatedly noticed how susceptible the

Leader was to pretty women and how quickly and skilfully he withdrew after his first advances.

Koehler goes on to claim that Hitler had been engaged to the sister of his first chauffeur in 1923. Her name was Jenny Haug.

> Hitler was already conscious of his perversion which excluded the possibility of consummation, so although he courted her and took her out frequently he politely took his leave at her door. Practical Jenny was by no means content with this merely superficial attachment, for she suspected that her swain must be intimate with some other woman and as a consequence shrank from making love to her more violently. Hitler was annoyed about this and soon broke off the engagement.

There is no evidence of this relationship, let alone an engagement, so Koehler's assertion that Hitler sought medical treatment for his alleged 'perversion' during the time he was infatuated with his niece Grete (Geli) Raubal must also be regarded with scepticism.

> The greatest attachment he has had for a woman was in his Munich days and this for his niece, Grete Raubal (who) took her life in 1930 [*sic*] out of grief for her Uncle Adolf's abnormality. Hitler loved his niece enough to think of wedding her yet he knew that his abnormality would make a marriage scarcely tolerable. He visited several well-known doctors and even underwent treatment which, however, was not successful [. . .] the various courses of treatment which he had undergone became public knowledge and were used by friends and opponents for extortion. This, and their actual relationship which was becoming

more and more intolerable, finally seem to have driven Geli to suicide.

The perversion to which Koehler and the other former associates allude is thought to be of a sadomasochistic nature, but such topics were not considered fit to print in the national press at the time. Even homosexuality was alluded to with coy euphemisms, so Koehler had to expressly rule out the obvious assumption.

> It must be stressed that the Leader is decidedly not a homosexual. All such rumours are based on the fact that it cannot be proved that he has had any normal relations with women. His sexual abnormality is of quite different a nature.

What that 'abnormality' might be was made public knowledge in 1943. The Berlin columnist Bella Fromm wrote:

> I rather believe, and many people have felt the same way, that he is asexual, or perhaps impotent, finding a sexual sublimation through cruelty. They take private films of an especially gruesome nature in concentration camps. Films that only the Fuehrer sees. These are rushed to him and shown, night after night. Occasionally Hitler's interest in a woman may be aroused; he may feel attracted by her charm, but that is all. His emotions culminate in a kind of jealousy caused by his sense of frustration, in the knowledge that he cannot respond normally. (*Blood and Banquets*, 1943)

Hitler is also said to have enjoyed a mild flirtation with Ada Klein, who worked as a secretary for the Munich publisher Max Amann in the late 1920s. She visited him alone at the Haus Wachenfeld and in Emil Maurice's rooms, when the chauffeur excused himself to give them privacy. Klein told Frau Schroeder that there had been no intimacy between them but that Hitler had told Klein that she made him light-headed and that she had taught him 'how to kiss'.

'I RATHER BELIEVE THAT HE IS ASEXUAL, OR PERHAPS IMPOTENT, FINDING A SEXUAL SUBLIMATION THROUGH CRUELTY'

Hitler's close Jewish companion

Hitler's rabid anti-Semitism did not, apparently, prevent him from enjoying the company and attentions of operatic soprano Gretl Slezak, who was widely known to have a Jewish grandparent but continued to star at the Deutsche Oper in Berlin, thanks to the Führer's patronage. Christa Schroeder recounts how Hitler looked forward to every meeting with her, when she would regale him with the latest theatrical scandals. In March 1938, on the Sunday before the Anschluss, Gretl invited her infamous admirer to a private evening supper at her apartment on the Kurfürstendamm, for which she furnished two large five-armed candelabras which she hoped would provide a suitably romantic setting. Sitting next to him on the sofa she stroked his hand but he shrank away saying, 'Gretl, you know that I cannot allow that!'

Christa Schroeder was present at this intimate dinner and though she left the room several times to give them privacy, she was certain that when Hitler left the apartment a couple of hours later, he had not given in to Gretl's advances. But Gretl would not give up hope and just before New Year 1939 she gave Schroeder a letter to pass to her 'chief'. The secretary didn't ask what it contained, but if Gretl was imploring Hitler to return her affections and trying to assure him of her discretion, it did not have the desired effect. As Schroeder noted, he could not have had a romantic relationship with someone in the theatre because they would have used it to advance their careers.

Geli Raubal

Hitler's one great love, other than his mother, was not his mistress Eva Braun, but his niece Grete (Geli) Raubal. While Braun provided companionship, idle amusement and relief from boredom, Geli aroused a passion that was to have fatal consequences for her and threatened to end the career of the future Führer. Her mysterious death appears to hold the key to Hitler's sexuality and his peculiar relationship to the young women he was attracted to.

Geli was the youngest daughter of Hitler's half-sister Angela, who had offered to move in with him as his cook and companion after his release from prison in December 1924. In the event, Angela remained in Berchtesgaden while Geli was given a furnished room in her uncle's spacious second floor apartment at 16 Prinzregentenplatz in the Bogenhausen district of Munich.

Hanfstaengl described Geli as 'rather tall, blonde [. . .] heavily built, somewhat plain and on the whole showed rather clearly her peasant background'. She was a cheerful, vivacious girl with an abundance of self-confidence but also fiercely independent and self-willed. And at 19 she was half his age. The similarities to his parents' relationship could not have been lost on Hitler.

At first she and her Uncle Adolf enjoyed each other's company and became close. But she liked to flirt with his young Jewish driver Emil Maurice, who evidently was keen on her, and she couldn't see what her uncle could object to. Emil recalled:

He liked to show her off everywhere; he was proud of being seen in the company of such an attractive girl. He was convinced that in this way he impressed his comrades in the party, whose wives or girlfriends nearly all looked like washerwomen.

Uncle and niece took long walks through the woods on the Obersalzberg, attended parties in the city and picnicked on the Chiemsee. But their talks soon became more intimate and were conducted in whispers so that the housekeeper Anni Winter and her husband Georg could not overhear. And then came the arguments. 'Uncle Adolf' forbade his niece from going into town alone, from leaving to study singing in Vienna and from marrying Emil, who had proposed to her without her uncle's consent. Geli and Emil wrote secret letters to each other – in one she despaired at having to wait two years as her uncle insisted. Heinrich Hoffmann observed, 'He watched and gloated over her like some servant with a rare and lovely bloom, and to cherish and protect her was his one and only concern.'

But it would seem that she didn't welcome his obsessive attention and the restrictions he placed on her movements. Whenever he was away on Party business he had her followed by the SA and when she wanted to buy clothes he insisted on choosing them for her.

One of these SA bodyguards, Wilhelm Stocker, remembered:

> Many times when Hitler was away for several days at a political rally or tending to Party matters in Berlin or elsewhere, Geli would associate with other men. I liked the girl myself so I never told anyone what she did or where she went on these free nights. Hitler would have been furious if he had known that she was out with such men as a violin player from Augsburg or a ski instructor from Innsbruck.

For her part, Geli grew jealous of her uncle's attentiveness to Heinrich Hoffmann's 17-year-old assistant, Eva Braun, who would be driven to Party meetings and picnics as she had been in his open top Mercedes, but there was also the suggestion that she was being pressured by Hitler into performing intimate acts against her will. Stocker alleged:

> She admitted to me that at times Hitler made her do things in the privacy of her room that sickened her but when I asked her why she didn't refuse to do them she just shrugged and said that she didn't want to lose him to some woman that would do what he wanted. She was a girl that needed attention and needed it often. And she definitely wanted to remain Hitler's favourite girlfriend. She was willing to do anything to retain that status. At the beginning of 1931 I think she was worried that there might be another woman in Hitler's life because she mentioned to me several times that her uncle didn't seem to be as interested in her as he once was.

Hanfstaengl also alleged that Hitler forced Geli to pose in the nude for 'pornographic' sketches and that Franz Schwarz, the Party treasurer, was entrusted with buying these back when they fell into the hands of a blackmailer. Schwarz was apparently responsible for paying off a number of blackmailers who had heard of Hitler's sexual predilections.

It was an oppressive situation for a young girl and it could only end tragically.

Mysterious death

At 10 o'clock on the morning of Saturday 19 September 1931 Geli's lifeless body was found in her locked bedroom. She had died from a single shot which had narrowly missed her heart and entered her lung. Hitler's revolver lay on the floor and was swiftly disposed of by a loyal aide. An unfinished note was discovered nearby, addressed, it is assumed, to her lover (the music teacher in Vienna). It ended, 'When I come to Vienna – hopefully very soon – we'll drive together to Semmering an . . .' This suggests that either she had been interrupted (she had been heard to argue with her uncle as he left the house) or

GELI'S LIFELESS BODY WAS FOUND IN HER LOCKED BEDROOM. SHE HAD DIED FROM A SINGLE SHOT

that she had been killed to avoid a scandal.

Hitler's housekeeper, Anni Winter, is believed to have overheard that final argument. She heard Hitler say: 'You say you have to go to Vienna? Is it to see that filthy Jew, the one who claims to be a singing teacher? Is that it? Have you been seeing him secretly again? Have you forgotten I forbade you to have anything to do with him? Tell me the truth now. Why do you want to go to Vienna?'

Geli then replied: 'I have to go to Vienna, Uncle Alf, because I'm going to have a baby.'

The *Münchener Post* reported that 'The dead woman's nose was broken, and there were other serious injuries on the body,' which does not suggest a suicide, but murder.

Suicide doubts

Geli was buried in a Catholic cemetery in Vienna, which would not have been permitted had she taken her own life. Furthermore, with the body interred in Austria there was no risk of the German authorities requesting an autopsy. Shortly afterwards, Father Johann Pant, the priest who had conducted the funeral service, fled to France. In 1939 he wrote to the *Courrier d'Autriche* newspaper. 'They pretended that she committed suicide; I should never have allowed a suicide to be buried in consecrated ground. From the fact that I gave her Christian burial you can draw conclusions which I cannot communicate to you.'

Geli had taken shooting lessons with Henny Hoffmann,

so she knew how to handle a gun and would not have shot herself accidentally. Had she intended to commit suicide she presumably would not have missed her heart and risked a lingering, painful end as she slowly bled to death.

Hitler's first biographer, Konrad Heiden, disclosed that a compromising letter between the pair had to be retrieved from a blackmailer by a trusted priest, Father Stempfle, who was himself murdered three years later on the Night of the Long Knives, to ensure he didn't reveal its contents. Heiden believed that the letter contained evidence of Hitler's masochistic desires.

In *The Gangsters Around Hitler* (1942), Otto Strasser suggested that Geli despaired because she could not do 'what he wants me to', although that may have referred to his demand that she remain in the Obersalzberg and forget her singing ambitions and her lover. Geli's mother was of the opinion that the relationship with Emil had ended some time before and that the man she planned to marry was not her singing teacher but a violinist living in Linz, who was 16 years her senior.

A later biographer, Ian Kershaw, doubts the veracity of the accusations regarding Hitler's alleged perversions, noting that they originate from dubious sources and that they can be traced back to rumours circulated by his political enemies and former supporters, who wanted to portray him as a degenerate.

However, Ernst Hanfstaengl observed a peculiar incident at the Schwarzwälder Café, which suggests that Hitler's relationship with Geli was not as innocent as it appeared.

. . . as they walked through the streets after the meal, Hitler emphasised some threat against his opponents by cracking the heavy dog whip he still affected. I happened to catch a glimpse of Geli's face as he did it, and there was on it such a look of fear and contempt that I almost caught my breath. Whips as well, I thought, and really felt sorry for the girl . . . I could not help feeling that her share in the relationship was under compulsion [. . .] there is no doubt that Hitler was deeply attached to her, although she acted very peculiarly towards him. She seemed to be rather cool towards him at times and manifested more fear towards him than fascination for him.

Hitler's 'perversions'

A possible origin for her fear was offered by Otto Strasser in an interview conducted by American psychiatrist Walter Langer of the OSS (Office of Strategic Services) in Montreal in 1943. Geli apparently told Otto:

> . . . that Hitler made her undress and that he would lie down on the floor. Then she would have to squat down over his face where he could examine her at close range and this would make him very excited [. . .] He demanded things from her that were simply disgusting. She had never dreamed that such things could happen. When I asked her to tell me, she described things I had previously encountered in my reading of Krafft-Ebing's *Psychopathia Sexualis* when I was a student.

It is conceivable that Henny Hoffmann had been pestered to do the same. Strasser made further allegations of a similar nature in relation to Hitler and Leni Riefenstahl, while film director Adolf Zeissler had been told by actress Renate Müller that she had been invited for a private audience at the Chancellery in 1933 during which Hitler threw himself on the floor and pleaded with her to kick him until he was aroused. Hitler apologists will of course argue that all of these accusations are unfounded and are no more than scurrilous Allied propaganda, but it is extremely unlikely that such strikingly similar stories would be told by a number of individuals on different occasions, plus there is the suspicious demise of Müller herself (who jumped 40 feet to her death before the SS were able to question her).

Could this be what Hitler's biographer and contemporary Konrad Heiden meant when he wrote, 'Hitler is the slave of the women he loves.'? (*Hitler: A Biography*, Zurich, 1936).

Whatever the cause of Geli's fear, it would seem unlikely that she would kill herself to be free of Hitler. It is more probable that she was simply suffocated by his insane jealousy towards her younger admirers and what Ernst Hanfstaengl called his 'twisted tenderness'.

However, in *Hitler and I* Otto Strasser was adamant that it was murder.

His brother Paul had let it slip during a casual conversation in the spring of 1936, when talking about their elder brother Gregor: '[Gregor] told me he shot her during a quarrel, that perhaps he did not realize what he was doing. As soon as he had done it, he wanted to commit suicide, but Gregor prevented him.'

Henriette Hoffmann accepted a less melodramatic explanation.

> He had so limited her life, driven her into a corner, that she saw no other way out. In the end she hated her Uncle, actually she wanted to kill him. She couldn't do that so she killed herself to hurt him deeply, to destroy him. She knew nothing else could wound him.

Shrine to Geli

Whether wracked by guilt or genuinely distraught, Hitler ordered Geli's room to remain as it had been that day. It was roped off and preserved as a shrine to the one woman, other than his mother, that he said he truly loved.

Hitler was visibly shaken by the death of his niece, but his supreme self-confidence could not be shattered. The day after her funeral, 24 September 1931, he addressed a meeting in Hamburg and showed no outward signs of grief. There were city elections to contest and a campaign for the presidency to plan. He was more concerned that the rumours of his role in Geli's death did not distract from the message the Party was attempting to instil in the voters, or taint his image as the one man who could restore Germany to its rightful place in the world. He would never again allow a woman to get close to him or share his innermost thoughts and feelings.

Hanfstaengl later wrote:

> His long connection with Eva Braun never produced the moon-calf interludes he had enjoyed with Geli and which might in due course, perhaps, have made a normal man out of him. With her death the way was clear for his final development into a demon, with his sex life deteriorating again into a sort of bisexual narcissus-like vanity, with Eva Braun little more than a vague domestic adjunct.

Eva Braun

Adolf Hitler was seduced by his own image and was convinced that everyone he encountered would be similarly impressed. So for Christmas 1929 he thought he had the perfect present for Heinrich Hoffmann and his staff – a framed photograph of himself in his military uniform. It didn't occur to him that Hoffmann had all the photos of his most famous client he could ever wish for and that he was only being polite in appearing grateful for another, albeit signed and framed. Or perhaps Hitler was thinking of impressing Hoffmann's pretty young assistant, Eva Braun, whom he had met that October.

First meeting

Eva Braun was then 17, the daughter of a Munich schoolmaster, and the very image of healthy Aryan maidenhood. The job at Hoffmann's studio had been her first after leaving a Catholic convent and she was still living at home with her strict parents. But when work was over she had little on her mind other than enjoying herself, which meant socializing, swimming and shopping. She was in no hurry to find a husband and certainly wouldn't have seriously considered a relationship with a man more than twice her age.

She told her sister that Hitler had been introduced to her as Herr Wolf, the name he used when he travelled incognito and that she had been aware that he was looking at her legs while she was perched at the top of a ladder searching for some files. She referred to him as an 'elderly gentleman' although he was only 40 and recalled that they talked about music and the theatre over beer and sausages while he was 'devouring' her with his eyes.

It was only after he left that her employer told her his real name. Over the following weeks Hitler would come into the shop and offer her complimentary tickets to the theatre or the opera.

He was in the habit of offering these to anyone who worked for the Party, so Eva thought little of it at first, but then he invited her to the opera alone and she began to see him differently. Her father was against it. It wasn't just the age difference, nor the fact that rival party newspapers had insinuated that there was something unhealthy in Hitler's relationship with his niece. Herr Braun simply disapproved of the former 'Bavarian corporal' and refused to take him or his party seriously.

But after Geli's death Eva wrote expressing her sympathy, slipping the note into Hitler's coat pocket while he was distracted. A few weeks later she accompanied him to a restaurant and thereafter was rarely seen out of his sight. Frau Winter had the impression that she was pursuing him and was not as innocent or as naïve as she liked to appear. He was as erratic as she was intense. She never knew whether he would be delighted to see her or unresponsive. Finally, in November 1932, she appealed to his sense of melodrama by feigning a suicide attempt. It was such an obvious ploy to gain his attention – she shot herself in the throat yet managed to telephone Hitler's doctor – but he responded as she had planned by promising never to neglect her again.

Eva's friend Marion Schönmann, who was a witness to the event, told Christa Schroeder that it had been staged to ensure Hitler's attention. Heinrich Hoffmann's wife, Erna, had even used her make-up skills to give Eva a 'distressed' and pallid appearance in preparation for the couple's fraught reunion.

Hitler's indifference

But despite his promises, weeks went by without a letter or phone call from him and then he would take her out and not utter a word to her, being completely oblivious to her presence. She confided her feelings to her diary like the lovesick schoolgirl that she was.

On 6 February 1935, her twenty-third birthday, she wrote that she would have to learn patience as he had failed to turn up but had sent flowers instead of the puppy she had asked for.

Five days later she was 'infinitely happy' because he had promised to buy her a house, but on 4 March she was 'mortally unhappy again' because he had failed to visit her after promising that he would. She blamed herself for having nagged him for permission to attend a ball and then assumed that his failure to say goodbye before he set out on a long trip was his way of punishing her for pressuring him into allowing her to go. It didn't occur to her that he simply didn't care for her, or anyone else, and that her feelings were of no interest or concern to him. After being forbidden to write to him – presumably because he needed to keep their relationship a secret, or perhaps he didn't want to be bothered with her lovesick letters while he was campaigning – she wrote, 'Why doesn't he have done with me instead of tormenting me?'

When he finally returned, she spent three hours at his side in the Ritz-Carlton without a word from him while he sat besotted by actress Anny Ondra. At the end of the evening he gave her some money but she was not consoled. 'There were days last week when I cried every night as I accepted my "duty".'

On 10 May she bemoaned her fate: 'That he should have so little understanding and allow me to be humiliated in front of strangers.' Again she threatened suicide and on 28 May, after he failed to take her threat seriously, she took an overdose of Veronal which had the desired effect. Her sister found her in plenty of time to have her stomach pumped and Hitler relented, agreeing to buy her an apartment of her own on the Widenmayerstrasse, where he could visit in secret, and later a small house at 12 Wasserburger Strasse, so that she could leave Hoffmann's employ and play Hausfrau to 'the greatest man in Germany and the whole world'. But being Hitler's mistress required a special degree of servility and the ability to suffer in silence. Fortunately for her, Eva Braun was temperamentally suited for the job.

Secret relationship

Eva was devoted, obedient and undemanding. All she asked for was Hitler's assurance that he would love no other woman. It was a promise he found easy to make and to keep. She accepted that she would have to remain in the shadows for much of the time when they had company and retire to her room whenever he entertained official visitors. It was part of a politician's life, she told herself, and every girl in Germany would envy her, if only they knew. She understood the need to keep their relationship a secret from the German public for fear of disappointing his female admirers. She liked the idea of being his secret lover. It appealed to her schoolgirl fantasies. However, she was less keen on his strict paternal rules. He forbade her to use make-up, smoke in his presence, wear fashionable clothes or cavort in her swimwear when performing her daily exercises.

One of Hitler's personal secretaries, Traudl Junge, was startled when she met Eva Braun for the first time and saw the contrast between what Hitler had described as the ideal woman and the modern girl who flitted and fussed around him.

> She wasn't at all the kind of ideal German girl you saw on recruiting posters for the BdM [*League of German Girls*] or in the women's magazines. Her carefully done hair was bleached, and her pretty face was made up quite heavily. When I first saw her she was wearing a Nile-green dress of heavy woollen fabric. Its top fitted closely, and it had a bell-shaped skirt with a broad leopard skin edging at the hem . . . The dress had close-fitting sleeves, with two gold-coloured clips at its sweet-heart neckline.

It was galling for Eva to be forbidden from socializing with the other Nazi wives. But she suffered his 'eccentricities', the frequent humiliations of being spoken about as if she wasn't present and the gifts of cash given openly as if she was the housekeeper. She told herself that he didn't mean to be insensitive, that he was preoccupied and that he too was making sacrifices to rebuild Germany into an empire that would last a thousand years. But for a man who aspired to emulate Bismarck, Charlemagne and Napoleon, and oversee the construction of a new capital designed on a grand scale, he thought little of the people who supported him. Hitler treated Eva, his most loyal devotee, worse than his pet dog, rewarding her fidelity with cheap jewellery on those rare occasions when he condescended to buy her a present at all, and speaking about her in the most derogatory terms while she stood just inches away. 'A highly intelligent man should take a primitive and stupid woman' was only one of the many hurtful statements made in her presence.

Eva, meanwhile, consoled herself by poring over film magazines, reading crime novels, gossiping with friends about the lives and star signs of her screen idols and shopping. She also wallowed in the melancholy ballads made popular by Mimi Thoma, whose records she would play repeatedly, and she amused herself by teaching her caged bullfinch to whistle her favourite songs. She changed her clothes several times a day and played hostess to her friends in her private apartment until Hitler's guests had gone. Then she would appear, fluttering like a young bride who had been parted from her husband for too long.

Ribbentrop's aide, Reinhard Spitzy, was 'shocked' at how familiar she was when she burst in on them to announce that it was time for lunch. Others found her refreshing and natural, but for ministers and other government officials she appeared ill-suited and of low social status. But Hitler was not comfortable with educated, independently minded women. He needed to relax with a simple unpretentious girl who would bring him tea and cream cakes and fuss around him like a Hausfrau with nothing more on her mind than the price of her latest dress. Her preoccupation with fashion and film stars confirmed his views on women of a certain type. Traudl

Junge was astonished to see that Eva rarely wore the same clothes twice over the course of several weeks and that she changed several times a day so as to appear at luncheon, tea and dinner in a new outfit.

She would flick through the latest issues of glossy magazines for hours then rush off an order to her personal dressmaker in Berlin, Fräulein Heise, from whom she ordered hundreds of dresses over the

> **HITLER WAS NOT COMFORTABLE WITH EDUCATED, INDEPENDENTLY MINDED WOMEN. HE NEEDED TO RELAX WITH A SIMPLE UNPRETENTIOUS GIRL**

course of a few years. Some of these were adapted from the clothes she had seen in the magazines, while others were purchased direct from the designers. Even her lingerie was handmade and embroidered with her initials.

Life at the Berghof was similar to the scene in Orson Welles' film *Citizen Kane* (1941) where the publishing magnate's wife passes the time putting jigsaw puzzles together in a massive echoing living room that she compares to a mausoleum. There was nothing about Hitler's mountain sanctuary that could be described as 'intimate', which is not surprising given Hitler's preference for solemn grandeur in all things architectural (which Speer described as 'ocean liner-style'), and this included his relationship with Eva. Hitler's valet, Herbert Döhring, noted the formal manner in which Hitler greeted Braun each morning. 'It was not a love affair – never . . . it was a friendship – a forced, necessary one.'

Loyal to the end

Heinrich Hoffmann asserted that their relationship had been purely platonic, while several close associates of Braun confided to others that there was no physical element to the relationship. Julius Schaub, Hitler's Chief Adjutant, told an Allied interrogator that Hitler did not love her but was merely fond of her, while Christa Schroeder described their relationship as 'a façade' and believed that Hitler only kept her close because he could not afford another scandal if she attempted suicide again.

When Braun was attracted to Waffen-SS officer Hermann Fegelein, she admitted to Marion Schönmann that she could have fallen in love with him if only she had met him ten years earlier. 'A few years ago the boss said that if I fell in love one day with another man, then I should let him know and he would release me.' Evidently, Hitler did not have strong feelings towards the woman others regarded as his mistress. When Fegelein later married her sister Gretl, Eva inadvertently revealed her own sense of worthlessness. 'Now I am somebody,' she gushed, 'I am the sister-in-law of Fegelein!'

Hitler's sister Angela found Eva superficial and irritating in the extreme. Angela couldn't bear the thought of her daughter's memory being sullied by the presence of such a flighty, immature woman and left her brother's house for good. Christa Schroeder was convinced that Angela's departure was the result of her failed attempts to discredit Eva, which had backfired. Angela and the other women who had conspired to have Eva removed by sowing stories about her vanity were ordered to leave the Berghof.

Eva may have been shallow and self-centred, but when Goering and Himmler deserted him she remained by his side to the bitter end, loyal and subservient to the very last.

Hoffmann had described her as 'just an attractive little thing, in whom, in spite of her inconsequential and feather-brained outlook, he found the type of relaxation and repose he sought', while Hitler's nurse Erna Flegel, who witnessed the final days in the bunker in Berlin, remembered her as 'a completely colourless personality', whose death affected the survivors less than that of Blondi, Hitler's dog. Albert Speer was only moderately more charitable when he wrote, 'For all writers of history, Eva Braun is going to be a disappointment.'

CHAPTER TWO

The Feminine Side

The German voter's feminine side was constantly being appealed to, either by Hitler or by the woman who could have taken his place

It is customary to attribute the slavish adoration commonly exhibited by Hitler's more ardent female admirers to the release of repressed sexual energy and while that might seem highly improbable, a study of the wide-eyed, ecstatic faces in the numerous photographs and footage of Nazi rallies suggests that he had aroused something primal and instinctive in their nature.

Mass hysteria

Many of Hitler's public appearances were very skilfully orchestrated with dramatic lighting, rousing martial music and mass displays of choreographed pageantry, to whip up feverish excitement in the crowd in anticipation of the leader's entrance. His appearance would be deliberately delayed to create a level of expectation that was close to hysteria and his speeches were structured to build from a seductive undertone to an ecstatic climax. At this point the mob were permitted to release their pent-up passion with shouts of '*Sieg Heil*' and to demonstrate their allegiance by giving the rigid fascist salute. Meanwhile, the object of their adoration sunk back exhausted, drenched in perspiration, with a glazed look in his eyes and a self-satisfied smile on his face.

Eyewitnesses have testified to the rapturous effect he had on his female admirers.

Hermann Rauschning wrote:

> One must have seen from above, from the speaker's rostrum, the rapturously rolling, moist, veiled eyes of the female listeners in order to be in no further doubt as to the character of this enthusiasm [. . .] Women's gushing adulation, carried to the pitch of pseudo-religious ecstasy, provided the indispensable stimulus that could rouse him from his lethargy.

Similarly, Richard Grunberger, author of *The 12 Year Reich* (1971), observed that Hitler's oratory 'engendered a great deal of sexual hysteria among women . . . not least among spinsters, who transmuted their repressed yearnings into lachrymose adoration'.

HITLER'S ORATORY 'ENGENDERED A GREAT DEAL OF SEXUAL HYSTERIA AMONG WOMEN, NOT LEAST AMONG SPINSTERS'

The youngest of Hitler's private secretaries, Gertraud 'Traudl' Junge, acknowledged that the Führer was physically unattractive, but she believed that he exercised a charismatic power over women.

> It was more that he personified power – that was his fascination. And also his presence. He had a way of looking at you with those eyes, which could really set you alight . . . he gave off an aura of power, and that impressed women. Like a Messiah, perhaps.

The allusion is apt, for it was known that those women who were fortunate enough to meet the man they called 'the saviour of Germany' were themselves treated as special, as if they had made a pilgrimage to a holy place and had returned transformed by having been in the presence of something sacred. Little did they know at the time that the object of their veneration was a false messiah.

The American psychoanalyst Walter Langer studied footage of Hitler's speeches and concluded that he seduced his audience by unconsciously appealing to their feminine nature.

> In regarding his audience as fundamentally feminine in character, his appeal is directed at a repressed part of their personalities. In many of the German people there seems to be a strong feminine-masochistic tendency which is usually covered over by more 'virile' characteristics but which finds partial gratification in submissive behaviour, discipline, sacrifice, etc. Nevertheless, it does seem to disturb them and they try to compensate for it by going to the other extreme of courage, pugnaciousness, determination, etc. Most Germans are unaware of this hidden part of their personalities and would deny its existence vehemently if such an insinuation is made. Hitler, however, appeals to it directly and he is in an excellent position to know what goes on in that region because in him this side of his personality was not only conscious but dominant throughout his earlier life.

Men too, were swept up in the tidal wave of excitement, but it was the passion of Hitler's conviction that inflamed them and the belief that he was expressing what they had left unsaid for so long.

The disenchanted former Nazi Party member Otto Strasser summed it up by saying: 'He touches each private wound on the raw, liberating the mass unconscious, expressing its innermost aspirations, telling it what it wants to hear.'

But for objective witnesses it was a form of mass hysteria which filled them with foreboding. The British theologian Ernestine Amy Buller described her impressions of a Nuremberg rally in her autobiography *Darkness Over Germany* (1943):

> I was sitting surrounded by thousands of S.A. men and as Hitler spoke I was most interested at the shouts and more often the muttered exclamations of the men around me, who were mainly workmen or lower middle class types. 'He speaks for me, he speaks for me.' '*Ach Gott*, he knows how I feel.' [. . .] One man in particular struck me as he leant forward with his head in his hands, and with a sort of convulsive sob said: '*Gott sei Dank*, he understands.'
>
> My attention was attracted by the face of a young man who was leading the cries. His arms were outstretched, and his face white, as he worked himself into a frenzy. And when the Fuhrer came there was ecstasy in his face such as I have never seen and should never expect to see outside an asylum.

Hitler did not win over the masses by virtue of his oratorical powers or his charismatic presence alone. He simply voiced what the people wanted to hear, a venting of their real and imagined grievances and the justification for taking their lost territory back by force.

Hitler himself admitted that he consciously manipulated the masses and that the larger the crowd, the easier it was to influence and incite them to follow.

> The masses are like an animal that obeys its instincts. They do not reach conclusions by reasoning . . . The masses have a simple system of thinking and feeling,

and anything that cannot be fitted into it disturbs them
[. . .] what you tell the people in the mass, in a receptive
state of fanatic devotion, will remain like words
received under a hypnotic influence, ineradicable, and
impervious to every reasonable explanation.

Hitler was empowered by the demonstrations of devotion
and it has been suggested that the orgiastic nature of the
Nazi rallies provided an outlet for his repressed, unsatisfied
desires. There was certainly an element of Pagan idolatry
in the rituals and ceremonial rites which reached a peak
at the annual rallies in Nuremberg, an aspect that Albert
Speer stage-managed as Hitler's architect. Using dozens
of anti-aircraft lights projecting beams into the night sky,
Speer created a cathedral of light inside which the
invocation of Mars could take place.

These were not Dionysian rites in which moral
restraint was abandoned and sensuality satiated, but the
opposite – the awakening of what Jung called the German
archetype, which sought authority and order. In effect,
Hitler appealed to the group soul which was wounded and
humiliated after the defeat of the Great War and was ready
to vent its collective rage against those it considered had
emasculated the Fatherland with their punitive reparations
and demands that Germany be stripped of its armaments.
He appeared at an opportune moment in the nation's
history to exploit this resentment and focus it on the most
convenient group he could offer as a sacrifice for its
most grievous sin, that of having lost a devastating war.
The Jews were the one element in their midst who would
be sure not to fight back but go meekly and obediently
out into the wilderness, banished, to die like the scapegoat
of biblical times.

In this unconscious act of deliverance Hitler assumed
the role of priest-king, who sanctioned the killing as an
offering to appease the gods, atone for past transgressions

and restore his people's pride. And to do this he needed the women of Germany to agree, otherwise there was a risk that they would act as the conscience of the nation and persuade their menfolk to refuse to obey. Getting women to embrace Nazi ideology was therefore essential, especially as there were women and children to be put to the sword as well as other 'undesirables', such as homosexuals, Gypsies, Jehovah's Witnesses and communists – all of whom had been identified by Hitler as a threat to traditional Christian morals.

Attracting support

But it is a mistake to believe, as many academics have contended, that the Nazis were supported by readily identifiable groups such as the disaffected unemployed, the working class and small business owners when, in fact, their grass roots support was largely regional. The majority of Nazi sympathizers in the early years were in the south, specifically in Bavaria, and were staunchly conservative and largely, but not exclusively, Catholic. The Party's appeal to the latter is at first difficult to account for, as the Nazis made no secret of their desire to supplant orthodox religion with their neo-Pagan cult. But the Nazi doctrine of 'Blood and Soil' had been cynically created to circumvent any reservations that these arch conservatives might have had in relinquishing their allegiance to the Church, appealing directly to their 'traditional moral values' and guaranteeing their rural culture and ties to the land as sacred and inviolate. In addition, the Party fuelled the fears of staunch Catholics by accusing the feminist movement of advocating the liberal use of contraception and encouraging abortions, which they claimed would have an adverse effect on Germany's population growth. However, it has to be said that several Catholic women's groups actively opposed Nazi policy, including all attempts to persuade

THE FEMININE PRINCIPLE WAS TO BE FOUND AND AWAKENED IN THE GERMAN PSYCHE AND NOT IN ANY ONE GROUP

their members to join the Deutsche Women's League.

It is also over-simplistic to view women during the Third Reich as straightforwardly submissive and more emotional than men. This is a traditional stereotype, an assumption of feminine inferiority that was used to justify a patriarchal society. It was also endorsed by the Church, with its belief in Original Sin, which deemed that women were to blame for the Fall, the expulsion from paradise, and therefore couldn't be trusted in positions of authority and power. As historian Richard J. Evans notes in 'German Women and the Triumph of Hitler' (*The Journal of Modern History*, Vol. 48, No. 1, March 1976), 'There is nothing specifically female about these qualities, nor are they common to all women.'

Hitler himself acknowledged that the feminine principle was to be found and awakened in the German psyche and not in any one group. 'The people in their overwhelming majority are so feminine by nature and attitude that sober reasoning determines their thoughts and actions far less than emotion and feeling.' (*Mein Kampf*)

Once this myth of 'the gentle sex' has been discounted, it is far easier to account for the actions of female Nazi collaborators which have been airbrushed out of history.

But to attribute the Party's success at the polls in 1932 entirely to Hitler's ability to appeal to an unconscious aspect of the voters' psyche is to overlook the fact that both male and female voters subscribed wholeheartedly to Nazi ideology – illogical, unjustifiable and inconsistent though it might have been.

Radio was another significant influence on women's voting during the 1920s and 1930s. The Weimar Republic had banned political discussions on the air in the belief that they were weighted in favour of those candidates who possessed a sonorous voice. The ban left housewives largely dependent on what their husbands told them and what they read in the newspapers or saw in the cinema newsreels. After the Nazis took power the radio was used as a primary distributor of Nazi propaganda. German women of all ages and classes would have been a captive audience, because the dictatorship forbade them from listening to foreign stations under threat of imprisonment. At one point the regime distributed thousands of wireless sets taken from deported Jews to homes that didn't possess a radio, so that the Führer and Goebbels could be welcomed into every German household.

The female vote

'I am no friend of female suffrage. I am opposed to universal, equal and secret voting rights. What nonsense – equal voting rights for the professor and the dairy maid!' (Hitler to Weimar reporter, 1931)

Nazi Germany was Hitler's neurosis made manifest: a dystopian feudal society in which all the advances humanity had made since the Dark Ages were reversed and its accumulated knowledge corrupted to placate one narcissistic megalomaniac and his malign acolytes. And yet this repressive, totalitarian, male-dominated regime had been legitimately elected, albeit by little more than a third of the population. A sizeable number of these voters had been women, for whom the new administration would prove the most retrogressive and disenfranchising since the Great War.

> In 1924 we had a sudden upsurge of women who were attracted by politics . . . They wanted to join the Reichstag, in order to raise the moral level. I told them that ninety per cent of the matters dealt with

by Parliament were masculine affairs, on which they could have no opinions of any value. They rebelled against this point of view, but I shut their mouths by saying, 'You will not claim that you know men as I know women.' (Adolf Hitler)

The decision to exclude women from the leadership and executive committee was made official policy in 1921, despite the fact that many men had been radicalized by their wives, whose sense of social injustice was arguably more acute than their husbands'. In 1924 Hitler rebuffed two aspiring female candidates for the Reichstag, Frau von Treuenfels and General Ludendorff's wife, Matilde. Hitler's personal dislike for female politicians was made clear in a remark he made some time later: 'A woman who sticks her nose in politics is an abomination to me.'

Goebbels' low opinion of women in public life was revealed by his attitude towards his own mother. 'Giving birth and rearing children are a life's work. My mother is the woman I have so much respect for and she is far from intelligent, but so close to life . . .' On 23 March 1932 his diary entry records a reappraisal of women's roles, if only because the Party's policy on women's rights had cost them the previous election and they needed to win their vote in the next if they were to become the major party in the Reichstag.

The Fuhrer develops completely new ideas on the theory of women . . . Woman is man's companion in sex and in work . . . In days gone by in the fields, today in the office. Man is the organiser of life, woman is his helper and his executive agent.

Goebbels sought justification for his reactionary views by citing examples from the animal kingdom, seemingly oblivious to the fact that what raises human beings above the animals is the fact that they have developed the capacity to reason and reflect, and that applies to both male and female.

> It is the duty of women to look beautiful and to give birth. That is not as crude and outdated as it may sound. Among birds the female smartens herself for the male and hatches the eggs for him. The male provides the food. At other times he stands guard and fends off the enemy.

Anti-feminist policies

The idealized Nazi woman looked out wide-eyed and ever-smiling from countless magazine covers and propaganda posters. It was the natural Nordic look – a freshly scrubbed, peaches-and-cream complexion unadorned by make-up and a trimly athletic figure attired in the *Dirndl*, a traditional costume worn by Bavarian peasants. Its simplicity was replicated in the uniform worn by the members of the BdM, the League of German Girls, who were dressed in an Alpine jerkin, white blouse and belted blue skirt with short white socks and flat-heeled leather shoes, designed to erase all traces of class or individuality.

Avoiding American corruption

Nazi women were the very antithesis of the fashionable modern miss or 'flapper' of the 1920s, whose bobbed hair, pearl necklaces, knee-length stockings and short-sleeved dresses with dropped waistlines and plunging necklines suggested loose morals and screamed independence. Conservative Germans suspected such hedonists would corrupt their sons with their lascivious dancing to that 'jungle music' they called jazz, and that their drinking and drug-taking would ultimately drain the vitality from German youth.

The flappers and all that they symbolized were seen by male reactionaries as representative of the insidious influence of America, whose endemic immorality threatened German femininity. For this reason the Nazis denigrated high fashion and frivolous luxuries as decadent and implied that anything American was of Jewish or Negro origin and therefore un-Aryan. They closed the popular cabarets and jazz clubs in 1935, citing the political nature of their acts and the sexual deviancy practised by their leading performers, who were often men in drag and women in male attire. And local Nazi-run councils banned singing and dancing in public places, making the display of naked female flesh illegal. However, their public protestations of prudish outrage contrasted with their private indulgences. Male members of the Nazi elite and their mistresses continued to frequent illegal jazz clubs and cabarets and consumed contraband luxuries with the appetite of those who knew it was too good to last.

Every aspect of life was brought under the strict control of the administration. Even citizens' sex lives were regulated by the banning of birth control on the grounds that contraception had been a largely Jewish invention and the Reich needed more babies. Public discussion of the merits of birth control was banned, together with the advertising of related products, despite the fact that condoms, intrauterine devices and diaphragms had been developed in Germany during the 1920s.

Abortion, which was labelled 'a crime against the body and the state', was discouraged for Aryans and only permitted under exceptional circumstances. In 1932 there had been 34,698 recorded terminations, but that figure fell to 9,701 between 1935 and 1940.

'Kinder, Küche und Kirche'

The Nazi election victories of 1932 marked the death knell of the despised Weimar Republic which, though destabilized and weakened by violent dissent, had consented to give women the vote and equality in almost all aspects of professional and daily life. The Republic had made abortion legal and contraception freely available. One of the most mystifying aspects of the Nazi era is why the newly emancipated women of Germany willingly and enthusiastically embraced an administration which had made its anti-feminist views well-known. It actively promoted its positively medieval policy of '*Kinder, Küche und Kirche*' in the first decades of the 20th century, when technological advances and innovations were revolutionizing western society. It's almost as if the women of Germany did not trust themselves to take advantage of the opportunities afforded them and turned instead to the 'strong man' and father figure the nation had needed since the Kaiser had deserted them and the ailing President von Hindenburg had shuffled off into retirement. (Hindenburg died in 1934.)

SINGLE WORKING WOMEN WERE REGARDED AS SECOND CLASS CITIZENS BY THE NAZI ADMINISTRATION

It is no exaggeration to say that single working women were regarded as second-class citizens by the Nazi administration. Unmarried women were considered to be *Staatsangehöriger* ('subjects of the state') and were afforded the same legal status as Jews and the mentally disabled.

At the 1936 Nuremberg Party Rally Hitler denigrated the ambitious young woman who sought to educate herself and embark on a career.

> If today a woman lawyer achieves great things and nearby there lives a mother with five, six, or seven children, all of them healthy and well brought up, then I would say: from the point of view of the eternal benefit of our people, the woman who has borne and brought up children and who has therefore given our nation life in the future, has achieved more and done more!

Male support for the Nazis' anti-feminist policies can be attributed in part to the appearance of so many young women in the workplace and the realization that they could do many of the same tasks as men for a fraction of the wages. The call to *Kinder, Küche und Kirche* (which incidentally, was echoed by the Catholic Centre Party) would have appealed to their chauvinist prejudices and assuaged their fear of a feminist revolution, despite the fact that these jobs were often poorly paid and offered no prospect of promotion.

Jewish conspiracy fears

A substantial proportion of male voters were convinced that the women's movement was yet another facet of an international Jewish conspiracy created to undermine the family and destabilize society and they looked to the Nazi Party to put women 'back in their place'. As Richard J. Evans observed, for these men the women's movement was 'spreading the "feminine" doctrines of pacifism, democracy and "materialism"'.

Of course, Hitler could not be heard to speak out against women's rights if he wanted to secure their vote, so he condemned the emancipation movement as nothing more than a 'front' for the mythical international Jewish conspiracy and therefore something no decent German woman would subscribe to.

> The so-called granting of equal rights to women, which Marxism demands in reality does not grant equal rights but constitutes a deprivation of rights, since it draws the woman into an area in which she will necessarily be inferior. (Adolf Hitler)

Consequently, the newly liberated women may have felt resentful rather than grateful for the 'new opportunities' and might have voted for the Nazis in the belief that they couldn't be any worse than the current administration, an attitude that was not confined to Germany in the interwar years.

The Nazis assumed, as did their political rivals and the vast majority of the male population, that women were not interested in politics or current affairs, but only in 'women's issues' and the immediate needs of their families (despite the fact that 112 German women were elected to the Reichstag between 1919 and 1932).

Women's vote

Even poorly educated, working class males imagined they had a rudimentary grasp of politics and the right to voice their opinion, while women of all classes were assumed to be preoccupied with more practical problems – namely feeding the family and clothing the children. But this myth was shattered with the onset of the Depression in 1929, which affected young single women more than their male counterparts. An entire generation had their expectations of financial independence shaken by sudden redundancy, economic uncertainty and the realization that even if their employment was secure there was little or no hope of advancement. Their bitter disillusionment with the broken promises of the Weimar government would have driven many to support a party whose promise of 'work and bread' (a key slogan in Nazi campaigns) would have been sufficient to persuade them to give the National Socialists a chance, despite their 'extremist' policies.

Contrary to popular perception, women did not vote in greater numbers for the Nazis than for any of the rival parties. In the presidential election of 13 March 1933, for example, Hindenburg attracted more women supporters than Hitler (51.6 per cent of the female votes went to Hindenburg as opposed to 26.5 per cent for Hitler in the first round; in the second Hindenburg obtained 56 per cent of the female votes while Hitler accumulated just 33.6 per cent).

Although the Party set out to reassure wavering voters in the March 1933 election that they regarded women as the 'equal of men in political life' – and Frau Goebbels had been persuaded to deny reports in the foreign press that women had been excluded from the professions – the Nazis relentlessly hammered home the idea that the restoration of Germany lay in the hands of its menfolk. Steely determination, the threat of military action and grim resolve were needed to wrest the 'stolen' territories back from the victors of Versailles, to push through the massive programme of public works and put German industry back on its feet. There could be no place in this strenuous undertaking for women except behind the lines in the service industries, in the home looking after the children and attending church services to implore God to remain on their side during the struggle. A 'strong leader' would have to be entrusted with this onerous task, a man who could emulate the 'Iron Chancellor', Otto von Bismarck, and who would restore Germany's pride.

The female Führers

Elsbeth Zander

If Adolf Hitler had not appeared to lead the NSDAP in 1921, Germany might have fallen in line behind Elsbeth Zander, a stern-faced, middle-aged former domestic science teacher who became a Nazi agitator with a rabble-rousing oratory to match that of the Führer himself.

In 1923 she founded the Order of the Red Swastika, whose symbol combined the Hakenkreuz of National Socialism with the Red Cross of humanitarianism to indicate that she and her sisterhood of brown nurses intended to care for homeless and sick SA men. Her 13,000 members saw their role as surrogate mothers for impoverished storm troopers and their families, for whom they cooked a weekly meal and did the laundry. But although Zander cultivated an image of the radicalized working class Hausfrau and loyal acolyte tirelessly campaigning for the cause, she secretly nurtured a burning ambition to lead a personality cult of her own.

She published her own newspaper, *The German Woman's Service and Sacrifice*, as an organ for her personal attacks on Germany's enemies, which were not always those targeted by the Party. Communists were condemned for defeminizing women by urging them to join the labour force, but she was equally disparaging of socialites who frittered away their energies in frivolous pursuits, a tactic which incensed the Nazi hierarchy whose wives regularly came in for Zander's scathing criticism. Her one-woman moral crusade to restore 'traditional family values' won her a loyal and fanatical following, whose members praised her in verse in the pages of her own newspaper and led processions proclaiming her arrival during her speaking tours, but she refrained from condemning Julius Streicher's pornographic rag, *Der Stürmer*, because she knew its publisher had Hitler's approval.

Initially, she served the Party well, rationalizing its prohibition of women in the workplace by arguing that women only worked from necessity not personal ambition and that the work was often routine and unfulfilling. Better that they purify themselves in the 'holy flame of mother-hood'. Defending the exclusion of women from politics and public life, Zander declared that the 'turmoil' of politics was not for the German woman, whose natural sphere was the 'social domain' and whose true profession was motherhood. Women should nevertheless acquaint themselves with major political issues and familiarize them-selves with the laws that affected family life.

But her more militant followers were not satisfied with tending the wounded SA thugs or serving soup to their families. They visualized themselves storming the barricades in a violent struggle against communism and fending off the forces of law and order, which they accused of victimizing and harassing the storm troopers. They decided that they merited a more revolutionary name in keeping with their contribution – for had they not endured verbal abuse and barracking from their fellow citizens, who called them 'Hitler's whores', dodged stones when they marched through the streets and hid weapons for the men under their skirts when the police searched them?

In honour of their participation in the 'struggle' they named themselves the 'Army of the Red Swastika' and abandoned their charitable activities in favour of active support for the SA.

In 1926 Zander received official recognition as the national leader of the Nazi women's movement, officially known as the Women's Order, but her arrogant disregard for Party regulations was already arousing the ire of her colleagues, who accused her of refusing to keep up-to-date records and wasting funds on lavish meals for herself and her staff. She was also criticized for refusing to delegate and of allowing the Berlin rest centre to operate without supervision, under the pretext that her role was to recruit new members, not oversee the day-to-day running of the organization. This complacency frustrated her assistants so much that they complained to the Brown House (the Nazi Party headquarters in Munich), who instigated an official investigation and discovered that her extravagance had resulted in the organization falling into debt, despite the increasing membership, and had generated low morale among the staff. Her brown nurses were reproved for their lack of training and absence of basic skills and Zander herself was described as 'psychopathological'.

The leadership were inclined to dismiss her despite her usefulness as a recruiter, while Goebbels considered prosecuting her in the courts to recover the misappropriated funds. However, reason eventually prevailed and a typical Nazi solution was found to resolve the problem and save face all round – and the attendant bad publicity. Party strategist Gregor Strasser suggested dissolving Zander's organization and making her the symbolic leader of a new body, the National Socialist Women's Organization, or *Frauenschaft*, which would be strictly controlled by the Brown House.

Guida Diehl

Zander's frenzied rhetoric had appealed primarily to working class women with little or no education, who heard their own anger and frustration expressed in her impassioned speeches and who shared her impatience for revolution. But there were also women who were less militant but no less intense and persuasive, who took the National Socialist message to the more affluent neighbourhoods. They used reasoned arguments to persuade the more serious-minded middle class women that the Party offered the only sensible alternative to the current administration and the communists.

One of the most articulate but also the most pompous was Guida Diehl, a Protestant social worker whose inbred anti-Semitism drove her to evangelize on the dangers posed by the unholy trinity of American culture, materialism and the mythical international Jewish conspiracy. Germany's strength, she said, was being diluted by American culture, which encouraged women to abandon their natural sphere and seek independent libertine lives of pleasure and corrupted German men into indulging their feminine sides.

Drawing on biblical imagery and German legend she portrayed Hitler as the 'heroic' knight who God had sent to save the virtuous maidens and devoted mothers of the Fatherland from the dragon of international Jewry. Her prose was as purple and florid as any pulp romance, but it proved effective in winning over 500 women to her own extreme Nationalist Newland

Movement based in Eisenach, Saxony, earning her the title Hitler's prime evangelist.

Her organization predated the Nazi Party by five years, having been founded in 1917 to 'educate' women against the dangers of feminism – which, Diehl argued, advocated promiscuity, endorsed birth control and lobbied for the abolition of the abortion law (section 218 of the Penal Code). Its core programme espoused Christian morals but disparaged forgiveness. Followers believed that it was their Christian duty to stamp out lascivious behaviour such as dancing in public and decadent theatre productions, which promoted sex outside marriage. Its manifesto attracted members from the Protestant women's organizations and the BDF (the Federation of German Women's Associations).

Under Diehl's proposals mothers would receive state subsidies to remain at home, so that they wouldn't have to go out to work and leave their children if their husbands couldn't afford to support them. A firm believer in the partition of the sexes in public life, she proposed the establishment of a separate legislative forum run by women to debate health, welfare, education and family law issues.

By the end of the 1920s she was claiming a membership in excess of 200,000, although this is hotly disputed. Diehl delayed joining the Nazi Party until 1930, when she was 62, because she wanted to remain independent, but once she saw the benefit of marching shoulder to shoulder with Hitler she became a zealous convert, invoking the spectre of Brünhild, the female warrior heroine of the *Nibelungenlied* saga, in an effort to recruit more members. She wrote in *Die Deutsche Frau und der National Sozialismus* ('The German Woman and National Socialism'):

> The true German woman is a fighter, and a fighter out of mother love. For us women it was almost unendurable to see the weakness of manhood in

> the last decades . . . Then we called to German men:
> 'We implore you, German Men, among whom we
> have seen and admired so much heroic courage . . .
> Call us to every service, even to weapons!'

Within a year of swearing an oath of allegiance she was manoeuvring herself into a position to take over the Party, but was dissuaded by an offer to accept a prominent role as cultural adviser under the supervision of Elsbeth Zander. Diehl had no regard for Zander and would not consider relinquishing the leadership of her own Newland Movement. This brought her into conflict with the equally intractable and officious Kate Auerhahn, who was charged with formulating NSF policy under Gregor Strasser. If the Nazi leadership vied for Hitler's favours with all the Machiavellian intrigues of a Jacobean drama, their female counterparts proved no less ruthless and conniving. They marginalized their rivals by insisting that their pronouncements had to be vetted by their male superiors, denied them knowledge of official events, restricted their access to Party officials and ensured that their names did not appear in the Nazi press. Auerhahn employed all of these underhand tactics to isolate Diehl and render her ineffective. By May 1933 Diehl was prohibited from speaking on behalf of the NSF and subsequently faded into obscurity.

> ## IF THE NAZI LEADERSHIP VIED FOR HITLER'S FAVOURS THEIR FEMALE COUNTERPARTS PROVED NO LESS RUTHLESS AND CONNIVING

Elisabeth Polster

Nazi politics tended to attract obdurate, highly opinionated and officious personalities who were almost continually in competition with each other to prove themselves indispensable to the Party and earn the approval of their superiors, just as the bitter rivals within the Nazi leadership vied with each other to procure Hitler's attention. Male officials in the Party and the National Socialist administration operated within strictly defined spheres of influence and had prescribed duties to perform, so they could do little but complain bitterly and await an opportunity to disparage their enemies. In contrast, women's leaders had not been appointed by the regime, at least not prior to 1933, having either founded their own organizations or assumed command with their members' consent and so were continually diverted from their campaigns in order to assert their authority. In some cases, the bickering and backbiting forced even the most committed individuals to concede defeat.

Guida Diehl had been one, Elisabeth Polster was another. Polster didn't proselytize or preach, but persuaded the respectable ladies of Münster, where she worked as an assistant district leader, that Christianity and National Socialism were not mutually exclusive. She organized picnics instead of parades, arranged for city children to live on a farm during the summer and co-ordinated charitable activities to demonstrate how the community would help each other when the National Socialist revolution had been won. Combining her Christian convictions and faith in Nazi pseudoscience she embarked on a moral crusade to discourage incest among the working class, which she believed threatened to enfeeble the Aryan race. Her staff of nine and their 5,000 members volunteered to supply the impoverished with extra mattresses and blankets so that families wouldn't have to share their beds.

She could, of course, have accomplished this within a charitable association, but she chose to do so under the auspices of the Party because, like many other civic-minded women, she imagined that the Party was founded on National Socialist principles and would honour its promises to the less fortunate members of the community. She also wanted to align herself with its racist doctrine and sincerely believed that the impoverishment she saw all around her was not entirely due to economic factors, but had been visited upon Germany by insidious influences. Influences which had engineered the collapse of the economies of America and Europe in order to undermine society, the family and the moral fabric of the nation, thereby preparing the way for a global communist revolution. And that is why Polster and her female comrades threw themselves into Nazi community activities with such energy and enthusiasm.

Unfortunately for them, by the mid 1930s the Party was taking their allegiance and efforts for granted, expecting women's organizations to demonstrate the same enthusiasm and commitment they had shown in the early days of 'the struggle'. But many of the 66,500 members of Polster's National Socialist Women's Organization now had other obligations and priorities and protested that their fund-raising activities were being used to enrich corrupt Party officials instead of feeding and clothing the poor.

Disillusionment gave way to despair and despair to resentment as hardworking idealistic women realized that the activities they had formerly participated in voluntarily and at their convenience were now compulsory, and that meetings which had once brought them together were now being used to air personal grievances.

Family life suffered as mothers found themselves conscripted into undertaking more sales drives and attending fewer courses in ideology and motherhood, which they had enjoyed. They also objected to being compelled to sell subscriptions to Party publications and badges to poorer families who couldn't afford them, and who would not be enrolling just because they had been coerced into giving their last pfennigs for items they didn't want. While the Party's propaganda extolled the virtues of motherhood and portrayed a united nation, an increasing number of its most loyal members now complained of low morale and of unseemly interfactional squabbling, as one female leader accused another of disloyalty, prompting the accused to respond by threatening to revoke her rival's public speaking permit. It became farcical, with supporters neglecting their husbands and children to petition for the reinstatement of the blacklisted Irene Seydel, who had been sent by Elisabeth Polster to a national women's leader training camp for 're-education'. In a last-ditch effort to raise flagging morale, one of Polster's assistants proposed introducing a morale medal to reward members who displayed a cheerful disposition.

By the mid 1930s Polster herself wouldn't have qualified for the award. She had come to realize that Church and civic associations, as well as local branches of international organizations such as the Red Cross, had been paying her lip service in order to be spared Nazification, which entailed Party indoctrination and endorsement. These bodies had pledged allegiance to Hitler, purged their membership of Jews and elected Nazi-approved leaders to their committees to comply with Party edicts, but they refused to defer to Polster on internal matters, considering her presence to be an unwarranted intrusion into their affairs.

Matters came to a head in autumn 1935 when Polster antagonized Maria Jecker, a close associate of Gertrud Scholtz-Klink, head of the Nazi Women's Organization. Maria Jecker was the director of the nationwide Reich Association of Housewives, whose members had co-operated willingly with the Party from the start. But co-operation was not enough for Polster, who demanded that the president of her local branch in Münster, Frau Kruckmann, apply for Party membership or resign. When Kruckmann refused, Polster began circulating unfounded rumours about her effectiveness which incensed Kruckmann's supporters, forcing Polster to withdraw the allegations.

But then Polster became desperate to save face and drummed up a false charge she knew would find support at Party headquarters. She accused Kruckmann of disrespectful behaviour towards Scholtz-Klink, which elicited the desired response. Polster was given authority to dissolve the Münster branch of the Housewives' Association and in the process lost a sizeable group of pro-Nazi activists, who sided with their defamed former leader. It wasn't an isolated case. Within three years hundreds of local leaders and their members lost their enthusiasm for Party programmes, declining to attend education classes and refusing to support actions such as the boycotting of Jewish businesses, just to spite regional leaders like Polster who had forced their hand.

CHAPTER THREE

Women in the Fatherland

*Women rushed to the aid of the Party,
despite being betrayed by the leadership . . .*

Hitler gloried in the adoration he inspired among his
female followers, extolling their virtues as dutiful
daughters and self-sacrificing mothers of the Aryan nation,
but he did not welcome their active participation in the
movement he had initiated and he was vehemently opposed
to the idea of uniformed women marching in formation
behind his Aryan supermen.

At the 1932 Nuremberg Rally he admonished Baldur
von Schirach for allowing girls to join the parade, seeing
it as a mockery of his all-male movement. He only relented
when the Hitler Youth leader informed him that they were
determined to demonstrate their commitment and that
their exclusion would discourage women from working
for the Party.

Nazi misogyny

'The Nazi revolution will be an entirely male event.'
(Adolf Hitler)

From the earliest days of the movement the Nazis had
encouraged women to take an active and productive
role in promoting National Socialism and converting
their neighbours to the cause, but after Hitler's
succession to the Chancellorship in January 1933, the
Party betrayed its most ardent followers. Their energies
and abilities were squandered in fruitless mass meetings
that had no purpose other than to demonstrate support

for the leadership, or worse, their highly motivated leaders were replaced with minor male officials and dozens of proactive women's associations were amalgamated under one centralized organization which had no power to influence policy. And when its members expressed their concerns the regime made it clear that it would not tolerate dissent, invoking the Law of Malicious Gossip (1934) to stifle criticism, suppress free speech and make even the telling of jokes about the leadership a crime punishable by imprisonment.

As the leadership became intoxicated with power and increasingly arrogant its most misogynist members saw no need to moderate their pronouncements on the subject of a woman's role in the Reich. Nazi 'philosopher' Alfred Rosenberg failed to see that he was being both offensive and inconsistent in advocating polygamy and encouraging childless husbands to commit adultery in order to increase the population. It was not Party policy but a male fantasy, in which it was imagined that women would be willing to submit to men in uniform for purely patriotic reasons and that only by making themselves subservient to their male superiors would women find their true selves. As Vice-Chancellor Franz von Papen had expressed it, 'she who is not a mother is not a woman'.

'SHE WHO IS NOT A MOTHER IS NOT A WOMAN'

Housewives flock to the Party

And yet 34,000 housewives (mostly middle class and middle-aged) had enrolled in the Party before Hitler assumed power, despite the fact that no concerted effort had been made to recruit them, or even to address their particular interests. Of these the majority were highly motivated zealots who had seized the opportunity to convert their neighbours to the cause and to conduct their campaigns without interference from men. The lack of male intervention and supervision gave female activists the opportunity to create their own hierarchy within the Party and set their own agenda.

They might have been undervalued and unappreciated, but at least the Party's indifference left them free to organize themselves as they saw fit.

They were aware of the Party's aversion towards women in academia, the professions and politics, and still they justified their support by telling themselves that it was not necessary to agree with everything the Nazis stood for and that their more regressive policies would be modified once they found themselves in the rarefied atmosphere of the Reichstag. Such rabble-rousing tactics had only been used to stimulate debate and attract support in the initial stages of the campaign. Better to have reactionaries than revolutionaries in the Reichstag. Better an autocracy than anarchy. Once in power, it would be possible to influence policy and curtail the more rabid elements.

Feminist historian Claudia Koonz reasoned that, having been raised in a Christian household, German women, both Catholic and Protestant, had learned to filter out misogyny from a doctrine they otherwise regarded as sacred and to differentiate between the teachings of their saviour and those of his disciples. Besides, had Hitler not spoken of his reverence for women in general, and for his own mother, in such affectionate terms and with such candour that no one could doubt his sincerity? The irrational nature of fascism precluded the possibility of a leader appealing to the masses through the intellect. Therefore he had to arouse their basest emotions by appealing to their pride and their vanity, their love of country and hatred for their enemies. It was a crude but effective courtship to which even the most intelligent women were not immune.

'Why I became a Nazi'

The most revealing insight into the mind and motivation of female Nazi supporters can be gleaned from the entries submitted to an essay contest organized by sociologist Theodore Abel of Columbia University in 1936. Abel solicited entries from early converts to the cause (applicants had to have joined the Party prior to 1933) by writing to district party offices in Germany and offering a cash prize for the best essay on the subject 'Why I Became A Nazi'. In the following months Abel received more than 581 entries, 36 of which were from literate middle class women aged between 17 and 73, and though these could not be said to represent a random sample, it is generally accepted that they were fairly representative of the personality types who had been attracted to Nazism.

The dominant theme in 32 per cent of the essays was the desire to be part of an ethnic community spirit, the compulsion to conform and find like-minded individuals or risk being an outcast from a popular movement. 18 per cent identified Hitler as the personification of this '*Volksgemeinschaft*' (community spirit), but only 14 per cent identified their own anti-Semitism as a significant factor in joining the movement, while 23 per cent highlighted patriotism and a distrust of foreigners as their prime motivation. The group insulated them from their imagined enemies, whom they identified variously as foreigners, Jews, communists, capitalists, liberals and even Catholics. The few who thought racism 'un-Christian' and a 'religious issue' were persuaded to think otherwise by their fellow converts.

All of the women, bar the youngest, spoke of having been traumatized by their experiences in the Great War in which most had lost loved ones and several had witnessed brutality at first hand, leading them to express the wish that they had been born as males so they could fight for the Fatherland. About a quarter of the women had suffered a significant personal loss, usually the death of their father while they were still in childhood and they had subsequently endured long periods of poverty. This led them to join a party that offered them security, a shared purpose and a sense of belonging, giving meaning to their otherwise mundane and empty lives. In effect, the Party became their substitute family and the Führer their father figure.

Unlike the typical Nazi supporter of the 1920s, three-quarters of the women had grown up in urban regions and were reasonably well educated, though only five had pursued their education into adulthood. Significantly, 48 per cent of the total respondents (predominantly male) had engaged in violence themselves 'such as to imply sadism or masochism', according to Abel, and it was the opportunity to engage in violence that offered them the chance to cleanse themselves of their trauma or neurosis. But perhaps the most revealing aspect was the proliferation of religious language in the essays written by both men and women, which suggests that it was not politics, nor extreme nationalism that attracted these militants.

Words such as 'faith', 'righteous', 'convert', 'holy', 'heaven', 'blessed' and 'crusader' are sprinkled throughout the entries, with one woman confessing proudly to having made a shrine to Hitler – not an uncommon aspect of Hitler worship in the early 1930s – and another rejoicing in the fact that she had sacrificed her eldest son for the cause. 'How wonderful those years of struggle were,' she wrote, 'I would not have missed them for anything.' Tellingly one woman described her conversion by saying, 'You do not learn about National Socialism, you have to experience it.'

Hitler knew that he had evoked a primal longing deep within the German psyche when he declared: 'We

Hundreds of young women break through a barrier to greet
Hitler at the German Sports Festival in Breslau, July 1938.

Hitler relaxes in a deckchair next to his niece Angela 'Geli' Raubal, c. 1930. In September 1931, Geli's body was discovered in her Munich apartment. She had been shot through the lung with a bullet from Hitler's revolver.

The MV *Wilhelm Gustloff* was a cruise ship built in 1937 for the 'Strength through Joy' programme, a leisure organization established to promote National Socialism to the German public. In April 1938 the ship was ordered to set sail for Britain, where it cast anchor three miles offshore and was used as a floating polling station for 2,500 German citizens. They were ferried out to the ship to vote on the annexation of Austria – there's little doubt which way these women voted.

Josef and Magda Goebbels photographed in 1939.
Magda embodied the Aryan ideal of beauty, and was
presented as the perfect mother and housewife in Nazi
propaganda publications.

A photo taken from Eva Braun's personal album shows her and an unidentified friend at a house party in Munich. Braun hardly conformed to the 'Hausfrau' persona associated with Nazi womanhood – she enjoyed parties, dressing up, shopping and liked to smoke (when Hitler was not around).

Getty

Gertrud Scholtz-Klink, the head of the Nazi Women's League, is photographed during a 1936 visit to London. In 1978 Scholtz-Klink published a book, *Die Frau im Dritten Reich* ('The Woman in the Third Reich'), which underlined her continued support for National Socialism.

Lina Heydrich attends a concert with her husband, Reinhard, at the Wallenstein Palace in Prague in May 1942. Lina was a committed member of the Nazi Party and it was she who encouraged her husband to join the SS. He was assassinated a month after this picture was taken.

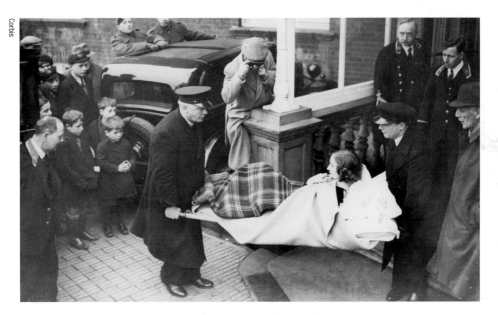

Unity Mitford returns to her home in High Wycombe on a stretcher after several years in Germany at the heart of Hitler's inner circle. Mitford allegedly shot herself in the head when she learned war had been declared between Britain and Germany – Hitler paid her hospital bills and arranged for her to be taken back to Britain.

Winifred Wagner, the daughter-in-law of the 19th century composer,
arrives at the Bayreuth Festival in the company of Hermann Goering.
Winifred ran the festival – an annual celebration of Richard Wagner's
work – from 1930 until the end of the Second World War.

LILIAN HARVEY

Czech actress Lída Baarová in *Patrioten* ('Patriots'), a 1937 film set during World War I. She had already been in a relationship with Goebbels for a year when this was taken.

Aviator Hanna Reitsch returns to her hometown of Hirschberg after being awarded the Iron Cross and greets well-wishers with a Nazi salute, c. April 1941.

Lilian Harvey was one of the brightest stars of the German screen during the 1920s and 30s, but her support of Jewish colleagues attracted the wrath of the Gestapo. She fled to France in 1937, then England, and ran a souvenir shop in Antibes after the war.

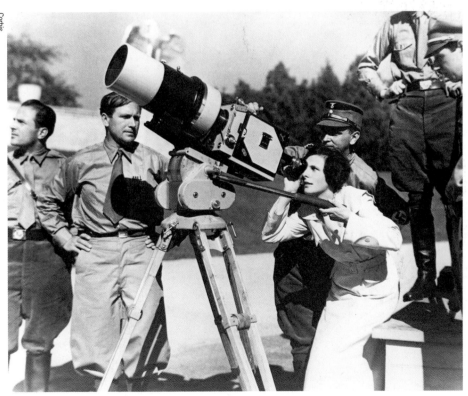

Film director Leni Riefenstahl shoots *Triumph des Willens* ('Triumph of the Will') on a street in Nuremberg during the 1934 Nazi Party Congress.

Swedish-born Zarah Leander became the star of the state-owned Universum Film AG in the 1930s and 40s. She was also a popular singer – two of her biggest war-time hits were *Davon geht die Welt nicht unter* ('That is not the end of the world') and *Ich weiß, es wird einmal ein Wunder gescheh'n* ('I know that some day a miracle will happen').

are not a movement, we are a religion.' (Waite, *The Psychopathic God*). It was this religious aspect of Nazism that appealed profoundly but unconsciously to both men and women and which accounted for such highly emotive responses from men who would normally not have given vent so freely to what they would have considered 'feminine' emotions. But Hitler had permitted them to do so, and in public, and this ensured that their devotion and their allegiance was deeper and stronger than a political leader or monarch would normally expect from his or her subjects.

Neither Franco nor Mussolini commanded anything like such reverence from their followers.

Equality hopes

Belonging to the Party absolved individuals of responsibility for determining their own fate and from fear of what the future might hold. They merely had to comply and all their thinking would be done for them. It was a question of faith, rather than political conviction. As with a quasi-religious cult, Nazism asked its followers to submit to a charismatic leader who would reward their unquestioning obedience by leading them to the Promised Land, only it would be to Pharaoh's Egypt in which they would be the masters and the conquered peoples their slaves. All they needed to do was to put their trust in him.

If there was ambiguity in the commandments of *Mein Kampf*, they assumed it was because they did not possess sufficient intelligence to interpret them and so they called for guidance and clarification on those points of doctrine that confused them. It didn't occur to them that the doctrine itself was muddled, contradictory, illogical and deliberately ambiguous because it was the product of an irrational man who spoke in absolutes and empty platitudes.

In desperation one rural activist wrote to her local leader asking permission to translate *Mein Kampf* into a language women could understand, substituting the title 'Our Struggle' for the original 'My Struggle', because she believed that the problem lay in the fact that it had been dictated from a male point of view. But the confusion and ambiguity worked in the Party's favour. Followers read into it what they wanted to, just as they had done with Hitler's speeches. With little or no substance pertaining to women's issues, they simply adapted Party rhetoric to endorse their own views and their male counterparts let them do so as they had no intention of fulfilling any of the promises or policy recommendations the women's organizations had made once they were in office.

As far as the leadership was concerned the various women's organizations were little more than Party fundraisers managing grass roots membership drives, sewing circles and public speaking engagements. The leadership had no intention of rewarding their female activists with anything other than profuse expressions of gratitude for their efforts when the campaigning was over.

Not a democracy

For their part, women's leaders expected the Party to discard their absurd '*Kinder, Küche und Kirche*' doggerel and be receptive to their recommendations in acknowledgement of the debt they owed to their female supporters. The leadership were aware of the women's demands, having closely monitored their speeches and read their pamphlets to ensure that they adhered to Party policy, but they had no intention of granting them. It was to be a dictatorship, not a democracy. There was to be no debate. No discussion.

Women had been informed of what was expected of them and they would defer to their male masters. In return they would be assured of the state's legal and financial protection and support. A strong woman radicalized by political activity was perceived as a threat to the Party hierarchy and, like an obedient child, should be seen and not heard. When victory came the Party would have to dissolve the majority of women's groups, replace its more independently minded leaders and establish Party-endorsed organizations under the leadership of women it could control.

Women are betrayed

After 1933 there were to be no more elections. The regime no longer required female activists to sing its praises and drum up support. The situation was summed up in a Party propaganda poster which declared 'The German woman is knitting once again', as if that was an achieve-ment to be applauded. But various women's interest groups were not content with vague promises and platitudes. They were impatient to be actively involved in government. Among them were a group of female academics who published a manifesto entitled *German Women to Adolf Hitler*, which comprised studious essays in support of Nazi racial theories as they applied to the sexes, in the hope of persuading the leader to reconsider his policy discouraging women from entering academia and the professions.

One contributor claimed that prehistoric skeletons unearthed in Scandinavia revealed that men and women had been of equal size and strength, but that men had starved their mates in order to subjugate them and, therefore, Aryan women would be the physical and intellectual equal of men if only they were permitted the same opportunities. But if Hitler was gratified to read that highly educated women accepted the more fanciful racial theories at face value and were prepared to suspend logic and compromise their credibility in order to endorse them, he wasn't sufficiently impressed to accede to their demands. He expected nothing less than total obedience and saw no need to reward those who complied.

If women thought themselves undervalued by the Party prior to 1933, it did not dampen their enthusiasm. They lived in hope that their contribution to 'the struggle' would be rewarded when victory had been secured. But even after Hitler's succession, when it became clear that the Party's hard line would not be compromised and that there would be no concessions, few women leaders raised objections to the purge of women from political and public life. None publicly condemned the dismissal of the 74 liberal and socialist female political appointees or the 19,000 female regional and local officials. Nor did they protest when it became known that all married women had been dismissed from their civil service posts and that women would be barred from serving on juries and practising law in the belief that they were not intellectually capable of logical thought or objective reasoning.

> **FEW WOMEN LEADERS RAISED OBJECTIONS TO THE PURGE OF WOMEN FROM POLITICAL AND PUBLIC LIFE**

Growing female support

On the contrary, support for the new administration increased so rapidly in the first 12 months that Party leaders were unable to decide how best to employ the number of independent women's organizations who rushed to offer their services to the state. Membership of the Nazi Women's Organization (the NSF) increased by 800 per cent and other groups obediently fell into line, pledging their allegiance to the new administration. If their educated middle class members had misgivings about Hitler's bombastic style and virulently racist rhetoric, they kept it to themselves. After all, had he not sworn to honour the role of mothers, preserve traditional family values, restore order and crush the Socialists? And still the restrictions and exclusions continued without a word of complaint from those who were directly affected.

Married female physicians were prohibited from practising their profession and soon afterwards single women doctors had their state-sponsored financial support withdrawn. Before the year had drawn to a close the number of female university students was restricted (to 10 per cent of total admissions) by a quota system, a move supported by Gertrud Baumer, a former Weimar government official, who agreed that it was a necessary step because academic standards for women had fallen under the previous administration. Whether she made the statement in the hope of securing a post in the new government is not known, although she subsequently applied for a position only to reject what was offered.

Divide and conquer

If there were murmurings of discontent among the members of the various women's associations they were not allowed to surface. Dissension in Hitler's totalitarian state was effectively suppressed by adhering to the proven rule of divide and conquer; giving similar responsibilities to competing departments and then having everyone defer to the Führer for final approval. The Nazi dictatorship presented a unified front, but behind the scenes reigned institutionalized confusion and interdepartmental rivalry. And this was the way Hitler intended it to be. He derived a perverse pleasure in seeing his subordinates compete for his attention. Being a man who placed great importance on instinct, he preferred to issue edicts on a whim like a Roman emperor and watch as his subordinates scrambled to implement them, with the added benefit that the responsibility for failure would be theirs alone and there would be no one to contradict him if he decided to distance himself from anyone who had fallen out of favour.

A similar strategy was employed to postpone decisions on women's issues and keep women's leaders at a distance. The once idealistic members now realized that their vision of an Aryan paradise of equal opportunity had instead manifested as a Kafkaesque bureaucracy administered by petty functionaries, all of whom were male with no interest in women's affairs. What they had failed to understand was that Hitler may have envisaged a Thousand Year Reich, but his immediate aim was conquest not culture. The needs and aspirations of German citizens were of no interest to a man consumed with the desire to wreak vengeance on Germany's enemies. His priority was the repossession of territory stolen by the victorious allies. He only paid lip service to the various interest groups in order to quell dissent and concentrate on the real business of the regime – rearmament.

At first the euphoria of election victory blinded female supporters to the fact that their backing was no longer required. Their considerable energies were being squandered and their input ignored. Women's leaders were excluded from official functions where they might have had the opportunity of meeting the Führer and lobbying on behalf of their members. Instead they had to be content with dealing with his minions: men like Gottfried Krummacher, a municipal administrator whose first official act was to abolish rival organizations and declare himself leader of the 'Women's Front' and its sister association, while proclaiming that he had been sent to 'pacify all of organized German womanhood'. Empty gestures were followed by empty promises.

Women's leaders replaced

Mass meetings were organized by Party officials at which thousands attended, but these served no real purpose other than to demonstrate public support and love for the Führer.

By the summer of 1933 it was evident to many women leaders that their efforts had been wasted, their ideals betrayed and their leaders replaced by male administrators who were 'worse than communists' (according to Maria Jecker, leader of the Reich Association of Housewives). Dr Auguste Reber-Gruber, head of the Nazi Teachers' Association, was moved to remark, 'Oh, how our old rivals would rejoice if they could see how badly the Party treats its women.'

At the annual Party rally in Nuremberg seven days were devoted to military parades, Hitler Youth activities and interminable speeches, but not one speech addressed the subject of women's rights or the opportunities that the revolution had won for them. Then Rudolf Hess announced the establishment of the Women's Bureau which effectively rendered all other women's organizations redundant and brought its members under the supervision of the Ministry of the Interior.

As feminist historian Claudia Koonz reflected, the old-time activists who had expended so much energy and enthusiasm in bringing the Party to power were excluded from the new organization because they had demonstrated the very qualities their new masters distrusted in women, namely ambition, determination and independence. The Party could not afford to acknowledge that women possessed these virtues, so they appointed a new figurehead to front the official Party-endorsed association. A woman who would do as she was told. That woman was Gertrud Scholtz-Klink.

'The Female Führer'

'The mission of woman is to minister in the home and in her profession to the needs of life from the first to last moment of man's existence.'

They say that behind every successful man there is a woman. And it is as true for dictators as it is for businessmen. In Hitler's case it was not his mistress Eva Braun who basked in his reflected glory, but the formidable Gertrud Scholtz-Klink, leader of the Nazi Women's Union, whose fanatical loyalty earned her the nickname, 'the Female Führer'.

At the height of her influence in 1941 it was estimated that she governed some 30 million German women and had command over 20 million more in the occupied territories. And yet there were those who described her as nothing more than a figurehead, appointed by the male-dominated and misogynistic leadership to give the impression that they valued the contribution made by their womenfolk. But she fitted in with the rigid bureaucratic Nazi mindset, being described by feminist historian Professor Claudia Koonz as 'Stubborn, simple-minded and self-righteous' and by American journalist and author William L. Shirer as 'particularly obnoxious and vapid'.

Run-of-the-mill beginnings

Born Gertrud Treusch on 9 February 1902 in Baden-Württemberg, there was nothing in her early life to suggest that she possessed leadership capabilities or ambitions beyond marrying as well as her background would allow. The daughter of a lowly civil servant, she worked first as a schoolteacher and then as a newspaper reporter before marrying Friedrich Klink in 1920, when she was barely 18. Although he was a minor official in the nascent Nazi Party and an active member of the SA she did not exhibit any serious interest in his activities or in politics until nine years later, when she had raised their six children to school age and was restless to pursue a life and career outside the home. On hearing of his death from a heart attack during a street brawl in March 1930, she marched down to the local Party offices and demanded to be enrolled so that she might 'honour his martyrdom'. Unsatisfied with organizing provincial party social events she soon graduated to recruiting supporters and became leader of the women's branch in Berlin.

Two years later Gertrud remarried, but was dismayed to discover that her new husband, country doctor Guenther Scholtz, had little interest in National Socialism and that politics came a poor second to his patients. But by this time her organizational skills and oratorical powers had brought her to the attention of Adolf Hitler, who subsequently appointed her leader of The National Socialist Women's Union and the Woman's League in 1933. Her critics, such as exiled newspaper editor Peter Engelmann, attributed her rise to her manoeuvrings behind the scenes, claiming she was as ruthless and devious as any of her male counterparts, while others believed that she was simply a strong archetypical Aryan mother chosen to put a face to the programme.

Preaching the gospel

Although she publicly ridiculed the idea of women pursuing a political career and denounced the female politicians of the Weimar Republic for making shrill street corner speeches, she threw herself body and soul into the maelstrom of party politics, relishing the excitement whipped up by the Führer's presence at every meeting she was privileged to attend. Her slavish adoration was absolute and brooked no criticism. With the fervour of the converted she preached the devil's gospel, urging all German women to surrender their personal interests and ambitions to the service of their male masters.

In a speech to German women ('To Be German Is To Be Strong', 1936) she made it clear where every woman's duty lay.

> The National Socialist movement sees the man and the woman as equal bearers of Germany's future. It asks, however, for more than in the past: that each

should first completely accomplish the tasks that are appropriate to his or her nature.

That year, in recognition of her unstinting efforts and initiative she was appointed Director of the National Socialist Welfare Organization and awarded the Gold Medal of the NSDAP, a singular honour reserved for those who embodied the ideals of the National Socialist state.

Life of luxury

But while she advocated restraint and moderation for her members in her role as head of the Woman's Labour Front, in private she enjoyed a luxurious lifestyle and all the privileges that went with her position.

She justified each extravagance by claiming that she worked tirelessly for her Führer, exercising control over every aspect of the female population of the Reich from adolescent *Mädchen* to matronly mothers. She could not bear to think of a single child lacking the 'protection' of the state and even set up a scheme to unburden French girls of the babies they had borne to German soldiers, with the promise that she would send these children to good German homes.

But she wouldn't be offering a home to any herself, having divorced her second husband in 1938 and acquired a third in 1940. SS Obergruppenführer August Heissmeyer was the head of an SS training school and a father of five offspring from a previous marriage. When the couple gave all eleven children a new home in Berlin and she gave birth to her seventh child in 1944, the Party praised her as a 'fertility model'.

Motherhood did not dampen her ardour for the cause nor see a reduction in her schedule of inspections to institutions and concentration camps, where female political prisoners were being brutalized.

At a camp near Berlin she found everything 'quite

normal' and 'in good order'. Her members were there in the capacity of 'social workers' assisting in the 're-education' of 'asocial' female political prisoners. One of these selfless women confided to Scholtz-Klink that they didn't have even the most essential materials such as soap, handicraft materials or playing cards and that the inmates were 'depressed' and expressed no desire to go home. Scholtz-Klink's solution was to order her members out and leave the rehabilitation of the inmates to those who wouldn't be so sensitive or distressed by the conditions.

Strength in defeat

If she noticed an increased eagerness to snap to attention whenever she entered a room and a tendency to follow her orders without question, would she have attributed it to her husband's position as head of the Ubergestapo, or Supreme SS tribunal? Or would she have imagined it was out of respect for her leadership of the Women's Bureau? In the event, she proved the stronger of the two, having been wounded five times during their breakout from Berlin in 1945 and later initiating an escape from a Russian POW camp, from where they fled to Bebenhausen Castle to be offered sanctuary in the village by Nazi sympathizer, Princess Pauline of Württemberg. When they were finally arrested by a combined force of American and French troops in 1948, Gertrud put aside the Christmas tree decorations she was making to sell and proudly admitted to having been a member of the Nazi Party, while her husband made an attempt to recover a phial of poison, but was prevented from taking his own life. He vigorously denied having ever been a member and swore blind he had always been a farmer.

A French military court sentenced her to 18 months in prison

> **WHEN ARRESTED GERTRUD PROUDLY ADMITTED TO HAVING BEEN A MEMBER OF THE NAZI PARTY**

for forging documents and in May 1950 a German de-Nazification court increased her term of imprisonment by a further 30 months and banned her for life from engaging in political or trade union activity. She was also prohibited from working as a journalist or teacher for ten years. On her release she returned to Bebenhausen and lived in quiet seclusion for 30 years.

Retired Nazi

In 1980 Professor Claudia Koonz of Duke University chanced upon a collection of Scholtz-Klink's wartime speeches and articles published under the title *The Woman In The Third Reich* (1978). It was stocked by a specialist feminist bookseller in Berlin who had refused to give shelf space to the highly regarded *The Feminist Movement in Germany* (Sage Publications) by historian Richard Evans, because the author was male, yet offered the former Nazi leader's title because its author was female, although one suspects political sympathies may have played a part. Crucially, its publisher had made the extraordinary and spurious claim that 'Without the courage, power and steadfastness of women, girls and mothers in the Third Reich the Germany of today would be unthinkable.' Its author had been allowed to dedicate the book to 'the victims of the Nuremberg Trials', by which she meant the defendants.

The book was to bring Koonz and its author face to face soon afterwards in the garden of her home in Tübingen, where the former Nazi leader was enjoying a quiet retirement. Physically she was still wiry and athletic and she remained as sharp and disingenuous as ever. Her practised evasions and stubborn refusal to accept any degree of responsibility for the crimes committed by the dictatorship left the American academic to conclude that her host's true guilt was her defiance in the face of the facts. Koonz found her arrogant, bigoted and unrepentant.

Her one regret, Scholtz-Klink admitted, was that she had been 'too busy' to master 'the intellectual underpinnings of the doctrine'. She admitted that 'some notions seemed extreme' but that they were born of idealism. When pressed on which notions she was referring to Scholtz-Klink became deliberately vague, replying that 'some of the aspirations were just unrealistic'.

Did she seriously believe she had influenced Hitler or the Party hierarchy regarding their policy towards women? Of course she did. She had 'enjoyed continual informal contacts with the highest officials', meaning that she had no formal meetings but managed to bend the ear of Goering, Goebbels and the rest of Hitler's gang whenever she bumped into them at official functions or rallies. She seemed oblivious to the irony of her statement when boasting 'Goebbels admitted he wished he had paid more attention to the women's division', which is to say that he hadn't treated it seriously when he was in office. Tellingly, she allowed Hitler to 'ramble on and on' before he had tired himself out, then broached the subject she had patiently waited to raise and hoped he would approve.

'We accomplished much in silence,' Scholtz-Klink informed her interviewer, which suggests that she had learned the value of listening and interpreting the will of her leader, rather than engaging in discussion or debate on an equal footing. Asked to give an example of a policy she had influenced she spoke of her refusal to allow her members to wear uniforms and volunteer for military service. Large numbers of German women were conscripted, so her influence was evidently limited. Her greatest contribution, she thought, was to instil Nazi ideals in every German woman and make them of one mind, while acknowledging that they had no influence over the male world outside the home. But her memory was highly selective. Scholtz–Klink talked of making firm friends with local leaders and yet their memos from the time reveal their suspicions of an interfering woman whose name they couldn't even be bothered to spell correctly.

Young Germans needed to be proud of their past, she said, by which she meant they should cease feeling guilty about the support their grandfathers and grandmothers had given the regime. The time had come, she declared, for all 'decent Germans' who had served the Third Reich to speak up and 'salvage the memories of their comrades who did not live long enough to defend their honour'.

Gertrud Scholtz-Klink remained a die-hard believer in National Socialism until her death in March 1999 at the age of 97 and she did so because she thought the regime had empowered women such as herself when, in fact, it had been a typical misogynistic state with all the power residing with the male elite. There were no female members of the Reichstag and no women were enthroned as heads of department other than herself. Women were active in the regime, but they were not decision-makers. As Professor Koonz observed after her interview with the female Führer, 'Here was the 19th century feminist's vision of the future in nightmare form.'

She had adhered to the law. Was it her fault if that law was immoral? Was it a crime to believe in perverted ideals? Gertrud Scholtz-Klink had evidently been as indoctrinated by Nazi propaganda as any of the Hausfraus and giddy young SS brides she had considered her intellectual inferiors.

Brides for Hitler

The lakeside model villa on Schwanenwerder island in a leafy suburb of Berlin was an idyllic setting for a summer school, but the *Reichsbräuteschule* was not a typical establishment for the daughters of Germany's reigning elite. Deportment and elocution lessons were not on the curriculum. Its stated aim was to 'mould housewives out of office girls' and to that end its all-female staff provided a comprehensive course in cooking, needlework and other mandatory domestic skills, with additional classes in racial theory and genetics.

The young girls who returned from the fields laden with baskets of freshly picked flowers might have stepped straight out of a recruitment poster for the League of German Maidens. With their peaches and cream complexions and their braided yellow plaits they personified the image of the perfect Jungfrau, but healthy minds and healthy bodies were not enough to make these daughters of the Reich eligible brides for their prospective husbands. They would first have to be indoctrinated in the cult of National Socialism if they were to serve their men as the Führer commanded and pledge allegiance to the Party and their leader unto death.

The villa, one of nine established in the capital in the late 1930s (with others in Oldenburg and Tübingen), was furnished as a model home with all modern amenities and the latest domestic appliances.

Surviving photographs from the era, which were published in the state-sponsored biweekly magazine for woman, *NS-Frauen Warte*, show a group of radiantly healthy young girls demonstrating the required skills; posing attentively around a sewing machine, tending farm animals, singing to an accordion and preparing a wholesome meal of meat and vegetables for their menfolk.

The Reich Bride Schools were the brainchild of Reichsführer-SS Heinrich Himmler and Gertrud Scholtz-Klink – although Scholtz-Klink was excluded from policy-making decisions, her face became as familiar to the German public as that of her superior. Himmler had signed a decree in 1936 stipulating that any young woman who wished to marry a member of the SS had to prove her National Socialist zeal by undergoing

HIMMLER TIMED HIS VISITS TO CATCH THE DANCING CLASSES AND WAS OFTEN SEEN OBSERVING THE WOMEN'S ATHLETIC ACTIVITIES WITH KEEN INTEREST

training to become a 'good wife' and the heart of the Nazi household. Only then would a marriage certificate be approved. But it has been said that Himmler's interest in the institution was not entirely political. He was known to time his visits to catch the dancing classes and was often seen observing their athletic activities with an unusually keen interest.

Rules for Reich brides

The role of the Reich Bride Schools might have remained no more than a footnote in history had it not been for a chance discovery of a rule book and other material unearthed at the Federal Archive in Koblenz in 2013. It revealed that the six-week course cost 135 Reichsmarks – a week's wages for the average typist or shop worker – and that classes were limited to 20 students who would be required to live in. They were urged to attend for two months prior to their wedding day, 'to recuperate spiritually and physically, to forget the daily worries associated with their previous professions, to find the way and to feel the joy for their new lives as wives'.

The topics covered every aspect of domestic life from basic household skills such as ironing, interior decorating and gardening, to handy tips for removing stains from their husband's uniform and making small talk at official Party functions. Great emphasis was put on child care as the aim was to turn out dutiful, hard-working Hausfraus and productive mothers who would breed blond, blue-eyed Aryan babies for the state – a duty that would be encouraged by a loan of 1,000 Reichsmarks to the newly-weds, with a quarter of the money to be kept on the birth of each child. The payment had been stipulated by the Law for the Encouragement of Marriage Act passed in July 1933 and in the first three years payments were made to 695,000 couples.

Girls were also obligated to teach the regime's 'racial values' to their offspring and to be the moral centre of the family, whose credo was to be adopted religiously from *Mein Kampf*, leaving no room for the Bible. This secular belief system was central to the New Order and was to replace religious observance in the Nazi household, beginning with the neo-Pagan marriage ceremony which would be conducted by a Party official before an altar decorated with SS runes and wreaths of oak leaves. The services of a priest would not be required.

The schools had initially been set up to attract the fiancées of SS officers, but by 1940 they were widening their selection process and relaxing their entry requirements to entice girls who would make perfect partners for Party officials and the SS rank and file.

Enrolment only declined when the war turned against Germany and women were expected to work in munitions and armaments factories to fill the roles of men who had gone to the Front.

Working women

The regime had trumpeted its firm resolve to honour women, but when German industry required more workers to replace enlisted men, its policies proved to be as flexible as its principles. Prior to 1936 the state had discouraged mothers with young children from taking jobs if their husbands were earning a reasonable wage and offered both financial and other incentives for them to do so, including state-sponsored leisure activities, household education programmes and ceremonial awards. They even applied a crude form of organized peer pressure, with the *Frauenwerk* organization under Gertrud Scholz-Klink frowning upon 'double earners' who put material gain before motherhood and shaming them back into the kitchen. But after 1936 the needs of the German war machine took priority and women were urged to put their children into day care if necessary, so that they could fulfil their patriotic duty and contribute to the rearmament programme (although women were excluded from working in munitions factories).

But even after the recruitment drive only a third of German women were in paid employment, a pitiful increase on the peacetime figure and 87 per cent of these women were employed in clerical posts, in catering and in retail. It was only now that Nazi women's leaders realized what little power they wielded and leaders such as Scholtz-Klink were revealed to be mere Party stooges, self-serving opportunists who were unable to defend their about-turn as anything other than political expediency.

But there would be no opportunity for their members to protest. The nation was gearing up for war and dissent would be considered as an act of treason. Women leaders saw no option but to comply and in doing so they rendered themselves complicit in the crimes of the regime they had actively and enthusiastically assisted into power.

As Claudia Koonz has noted in *Mothers In The Fatherland*, far from honouring the family as the heart of the *Volk* community, women's leaders had aided the state's intrusion into the home in order to control its members' activities, their conduct and even their thoughts. Mothers and fathers who dared voice criticism of the leadership lived in fear that their own children, other family members or their neighbours might denounce them to the Gestapo. But an even more insidious influence would undermine the traditional family in the run-up to war. In October 1939 Reichsführer-SS Heinrich Himmler charged the three million men under his command to father as many children as they could out of wedlock as part of their sacred duty to the nation, dressing it up in the florid language of the

Nordic heroic saga. 'The greatest gift for the widow of a man killed in battle is always the child of the man she has loved.' But he was forced to withdraw the order after condemnation from Protestant and Catholic women's groups.

CHAPTER FOUR

Springtime for Hitler

The Nazis used every available means of increasing the population, including 'stud farms' and abduction . . .

In the pre-war years Hitler commanded the admiration of many foreign dignitaries and the grudging respect of his neighbours. While America and the rest of Europe languished in the trough of despair as the Great Depression dragged on, Germany enjoyed unprecedented growth.

In 1933, the first year of Hitler's chancellorship, unemployment had been reduced by a third to just under four million. The following year a further one million found work as part of a massive public works programme, guaranteeing jobs for hundreds of thousands of men who were drafted into the building of the first autobahns, while the construction of new government buildings in Berlin was stepped up as Hitler realized his ambition for a capital to rival Paris and New York.

Germanophilia

The former British prime minister David Lloyd George could barely contain his enthusiasm when writing in the *Daily Express*.

One man has accomplished this miracle. He is a born leader of men. A magnetic, dynamic personality with a single-minded purpose, a resolute will and a dauntless heart . . . The old trust him. The young idolise him. It is not the admiration accorded to a popular Leader. It is the worship of a national hero who has saved his country from utter despondency and degradation . . . not a word of criticism or of disapproval have I heard of Hitler. (*I Talked To Hitler*, 17 November 1936)

By the time the Olympic torch was ignited in Berlin that year Germany was the envy of the world. Politicians, celebrities and members of the aristocracy posed for the newsreel cameras with broad smiles on their faces and voiced their enthusiasm for the new Germany. Charles Lindbergh, the Duke and Duchess of Windsor and even the young John Kennedy praised Herr Hitler, unaware of, or in some cases unconcerned with, the price that had been paid for such rapid progress.

The young JFK, no doubt influenced by his father, US ambassador Joe Kennedy (known to the Nazis as 'Germany's best friend in London'), wrote, 'I have come to the conclusion that fascism is right for Germany and Italy. What are the evils of fascism compared to communism?'

The unions had been abolished, strikes were illegal, workers had no right to demand higher wages, shorter hours or improved conditions and were prohibited from changing their jobs without permission.

And, although Hitler was given credit for the 7,000 kilometres of autobahn laid by the end of the decade, in fact the network had been proposed by the previous administration, which had spent more on new roads in 1927 than the Nazis did in 1934.

Unemployment continued to fall year on year but from 1935 this was largely due to the introduction of conscription, which saw one and a half million men in uniform by 1939.

The rural idyll Hitler had promised was a regressive feudal system achieved by the awarding of massive subsidies to farmers in order to keep prices artificially low.

Industry too was booming due to rearmament, which incurred debts of 26 billion marks, none of which Hitler had the faintest intention of repaying.

And as for the regime's record on human rights, none of the visitors raised the issue for fear of incurring their host's displeasure. There was work, bread and hope. Confidence and self-assurance had replaced despondency and resentment over the punitive reparations and restrictions imposed by the Versailles Treaty. Some might have seen it as arrogance, but there was no denying that Germany was strong again. So strong in fact, that the western democracies adopted a policy of appeasement to placate the dictator in the hope that each concession would be their last. Those who knew never to trust a tyrant warned of the dangers of acquiescing to each successive demand and of forestalling their own preparations for the war that was inevitable. But in the second half of the decade Hitler exercised a fatal attraction for many, particularly impressionable young women, who saw only the superficial glamour and gaiety of Berlin, the picture postcard scenery and the new spirit of optimism that was evident everywhere in the Reich.

A German education

During the 1930s many wealthy English parents sent their daughters to private finishing schools in Germany and the girls came back after six months singing the praises of the National Socialist state. One of those wide-eyed adolescents was the paternal grandmother of Rachel Johnson, sister of the future London mayor Boris Johnson, and another, coincidentally, was Rachel's future mother-in-law.

Both women were at school in Munich at roughly the same time

> **THERE WAS WORK, BREAD AND HOPE. CONFIDENCE AND SELF-ASSURANCE HAD REPLACED DESPONDENCY**

(April 1938) and witnessed the euphoria after Hitler had annexed Austria without a shot being fired.

Rachel interviewed a dozen English women who were in Germany in the late 1930s while researching a novel, *Winter Games,* and they all spoke of having had the time of their lives. She revealed her findings to the German magazine *Der Spiegel.*

> It was a rich experience, because England was very stuffy at that time – lots of unemployment, terrible food and nasty weather. In Bavaria they had the crisp mountain air, a healthy life, the opera, the mountains and handsome Germans in uniform. They couldn't believe their luck! No chaperones, no parents. They had everything, including sex.

She went on:

> Sending your daughters to finishing school in Germany was the thing to do. Germany was probably our closest European partner at that time. And don't forget that George V changed the name of his family from 'Saxe-Coburg and Gotha' to 'Windsor' only in 1917, during the First World War. There were still aristocratic connections and friendships to Germany between the wars [. . .] Some moved to Berlin or Dresden, but Bavaria with its mountains, castles, museums and beer cellars was more attractive . . . My maternal grandmother was in Bavaria in the 1930s, she was Jewish. She enjoyed the opera in Munich, skiing in the mountains and later fell in love with a ski instructor from Freiburg, a member of the National Socialist party. His family called her 'die Jüdin', the Jewess. Their relationship went disastrously wrong and she came back to England.

Although there were occasional items in the national newspapers and questions in the Houses of Parliament to raise public awareness of the plight of refugees, there was what Rachel called a 'wilful blindness' to the abuse of human rights in Germany, at least among those who wouldn't hear a word against Herr Hitler.

One of the elderly women Johnson interviewed told her, 'Hitler was marvellous, the problem was, he went a little bit too far.' Another told her about her Jewish music professor who suddenly vanished. His pupils simply accepted it.

> They weren't aware of anything at all. They would see a sign at a swimming pool saying 'No Jews', and they'd think: 'What is a Jew?' They didn't know any Jews. Also, they were upper middle class English girls, so almost by definition their fathers were probably quite anti-Semitic. It was an anti-Semitic time, not only in Germany. We had the rise of the far right, the brown shirts, and Oswald Mosley, leader of the British Union of Fascists. My mother-in-law's family was typical of aristocratic attitudes of this period. They were very pro-German. My mother-in-law's father was chairman of the Anglo-German Alliance, which was set up to bring the two countries closer together. He would make speeches in the House of Lords saying Hitler is a sound chap.

Unity Mitford

The most notorious of these acolytes was the society hostess Unity Mitford, daughter of Lord Redesdale, who Oswald Mosley had described as one of nature's fascists. Her father had given Unity the middle name 'Valkyrie' in homage to his favourite opera, Wagner's *Die Walküre*, and Unity had seen it as permission to decorate her bedroom wall with swastikas to torment her sister Jessica, who had communist sympathies. Unity's other sister Diana had married Oswald Mosley, leader of the British Union of Fascists in 1936 in the house of Josef Goebbels, with Hitler in attendance as a witness. But even Mosley found Unity's provocative 'exhibitionism' an embarrassment and urged Diana to persuade her sister to stop disrupting communist meetings, where she heckled the speakers and gave the Nazi salute.

But Unity was a die-hard fascist and follower of Adolf Hitler. She had heard him speak at the 1933 Nuremberg Rally and she was determined to meet him and ingratiate herself with him in the hope of becoming his mistress. She learned which Munich café he went to every day and stalked him until he finally invited her to his table.

'It was the most wonderful and beautiful [day] of my life,' she told her father. 'I am so happy that I wouldn't mind a bit, dying. I'd suppose I am the luckiest girl in the world. For me he is the greatest man of all time.'

Spurned affections

If she imagined that Hitler was attracted to her, she would have been sorely disappointed to learn that he thought her 'plain' and 'sexless'. Elmar Streicher, son of the infamous Julius Streicher, editor of *Der Stürmer*, recalled:

> She had nothing to do with Hitler as a woman, she was just a butterfly to a flower. As a woman she was so very tall, you had to laugh to see it. She simply wasn't sexy. She was a virgin to the day of her death, I'd put my hand in the fire to say that.

Hitler indulged her flattery because it pleased him to be pursued by a member of the British aristocracy and he would have been impressed by the fact that her grandfather had translated his favourite book, Houston Stewart

Chamberlain's racist diatribe, *The Foundations of the Nineteenth Century*, and had been a close friend of Richard Wagner.

Hitler strung her along because she would prove useful in influencing pro-German sympathizers back in Britain and by writing Nazi propaganda for British newspapers. But the Nazi hierarchy regarded her as a harmless lunatic and laughed behind her back at her habitual heel clicking and saluting every time Hitler entered the room. Her grasp of reality was certainly lacking if her reaction to the murder of SA leader Roehm and hundreds of former associates in the 'Night of the Long Knives' was indicative of her true feelings: 'Poor sweet Führer, he's having such a dreadful time.'

But Unity's admiration was not reciprocated and she found herself increasingly isolated after Eva Braun made another suicide attempt to secure Hitler's undivided attention. Eva's dislike of Unity was clear from her diary. 'She is known as the Valkyrie and looks the part, including her legs.'

Attempted suicide

Unity's passion for fascism remained undiminished, for which Hitler rewarded her with a gold Party badge and a private box at the 1936 Olympic Games. Her activities, however, were frowned on by British Intelligence, which categorized her as being 'more Nazi than the Nazis', while Guy Lidell, head of MI5, noted that her conduct 'had come perilously close to high treason'.

But Unity avoided embarrassing either side by attempting suicide on the day that war was declared between Britain and Germany. She shot herself in the head with a pearl-handled pistol that Hitler had given her, but survived and was brought back to Britain an invalid. When she was reunited with her family Unity confessed: 'I thought you all hated me but I don't remember why.'

She died eight years later, on 28 May 1948, supposedly from her self-inflicted wound.

However Guy Lidell suspected that the story of her botched suicide was a convenient cover story.

> We had no evidence to support the press allegations that she was in a serious state of health and it might well be that she was brought in on a stretcher in order to avoid publicity and unpleasantness to her family.

Goebbels on the role of women

On 18 March 1933, six weeks after Hitler was appointed Chancellor, Josef Goebbels was invited to open an exhibition celebrating women's contribution to contemporary society, at which he took the opportunity to reassure the women of Germany that their faith in National Socialism was not misplaced (source: 'Deutsches Frauentum', *Signale der neuen Zeit. 25 ausgewählte Reden von Dr. Josef Goebbels*, Munich: Zentralverlag der NSDAP, 1934).

He began by acknowledging that the Party had aroused fierce criticism for discouraging women from entering politics and then, in a characteristic example of Nazi doublespeak, he justified their exclusion by saying it was not from lack of respect, quite the contrary, the Party respected women too much to allow them to waste their talents in a field that did not suit the female character. Women were not inferior, but simply had a different purpose than men.

If the partnership of men and women was to benefit the state, women would have to accept that the female virtues of loyalty, selfless devotion and self-sacrifice would need to be applied to those areas of employment best suited to their sex and not those that are the preserve of men, such as politics and the military.

WOMEN WERE NOT TO THINK THEY WERE MISSING NEW OPPORTUNITIES IN THE WORKPLACE, THEY WERE ENSURING THE FUTURE OF THE NATION

Germany's recent troubles were to be blamed on the 'feminization' of men and the 'masculinization' of women, as the men in power had been increasingly reluctant to enforce the measures that were needed for fear of being unpopular. In short, the previous administration had not been hard enough, but now was the time for firmness and resolve, characteristics which did not come naturally to women.

What was perceived to be progress was not, in the opinion of the National Socialists, an improvement but a dangerous diversion which had given women false hope and distracted them from their natural vocation and duty, the nurturing of the family and the raising of children. Modern society was merely a façade, concealing the decline of the family and its traditional values.

Mothers of the nation

Women were not to think that they were missing new opportunities in the workplace, but rather ensuring the future of the nation by raising its new citizens with a shared belief and vision. That was not to say that those who had no children or who were employed had no less a role as 'mothers of the nation'. And the responsibility of the state was to support women so that they could fulfil their role; Goebbels assured the listening women that 'the national revolutionary government is anything but reactionary'. It was not opposed to progress, but it assumed the responsibility for its citizens by encouraging them to put their energies and abilities into their natural roles. More rights did not necessarily mean that women would be better off. The right to stand for public office was a bad bargain if it meant their quality of life was diminished because they'd lost the opportunity to be mothers.

Goebbels had appealed to their emotions. Now he appealed to their patriotic duty by reminding them that the birth rate had declined. In the major cities he claimed it had fallen from two million at the turn of the century to half that and that for the past 14 years the birth rate in Berlin was the lowest of any European city. It was not simply a matter of economics, but it signified a dilution or weakening of the nation's strength. Where there had been seven children to one elderly person in 1900, there would be a ratio of one to one if the current trend were to continue. It was a question of national necessity and survival. The new government would encourage larger families, though precisely how they would do that would be revealed in the coming months.

Lebensborn – sins of the fathers

The popular perception of the *Lebensborn* project is that it was a chain of Nazi stud farms where SS supermen mated with perfect specimens of Aryan womanhood. Although this was certainly one aspect of the programme implemented and closely monitored by Heinrich Himmler, the main purpose was to increase the birth rate in the greater Reich and reduce the high proportion of abortions, which had reached 800,000 per year in the early 1930s.

Unwed mothers would choose to abort rather than give their babies up for adoption or attempt to raise them as a single parent on charity, there being no financial state support for the unemployed in Germany in the interwar years. Bismarck had introduced limited financial incentives for the working man, to undermine the Socialists and discourage emigration, but single women were forced to find work or seek help from their families or charitable organizations.

In 1939 Himmler would write to Field-Marshal Keitel:

> According to statistics there are 600,000 abortions a year in Germany. The fact that these happen among the best German racial types has been worrying me for years. The way I see it we cannot afford to lose these young people, hundreds and thousands of them. The aim of protecting this German blood is of the highest priority. If we manage to stop these abortions we will be able to have 200 more German regiments every year on the march. Another 500,000 or 600,000 people could produce millions of marks for the economy. The strength of these soldiers and workers will build the greater Germany. This is why I founded *Lebensborn* in 1936. It fights abortions in a positive way. Every woman can have her child in peace and quiet and devote her life to the betterment of the race. (Source: *Master Race: The Lebensborn Experiment in Nazi Germany*, 1995, pp.66–7)

On its foundation in 1935 the stated aim of the *Lebensborn* ('Spring of Life') organization was to support 'racially and genetically valuable families with many children'.

Approximately 60 per cent of the women who were offered a bed in the maternity wards were unwed mothers who received the highest standard of care and the opportunity to give their baby up for adoption if they decided not to raise it themselves. The clinics even offered an SS christening with the children receiving a blessing under an SS dagger engraved with the motto 'My oath is loyalty', while the mother pledged allegiance to the Party. The service was provided primarily for the partners of married SS men who had fathered a child out of wedlock after being encouraged by Reichsführer Himmler to sire as many Aryan sons as they could. But the high standard of clinical care and privacy made it the first choice for expectant Nazi officer's wives and the men's mistresses.

Suffering the stigma

There was, however, a more sinister side to the *Lebensborn* 'adoption' programme.

In the occupied territories, local girls who became pregnant with the illegitimate child of a German soldier were left to raise the child alone after the war and endure the accusations and wrath of their neighbours, who damned them as Nazi whores and collaborators. The child would grow up not only with the stigma of illegitimacy, but also the anxiety of not knowing the identity of their father, who they feared might have been a war criminal.

Some endured abuse in institutions and in school if their teachers and classmates knew they were 'Nazi bastards'. In a terrible twist of fate many innocent children suffered a degree of mistreatment at the hands of their own countrymen similar to that meted out to non-Aryan children by the Nazis themselves.

There were 13 *Lebensborn* clinics in Germany and Austria, nine in Norway and others in France, Belgium, the Netherlands, Poland and Luxembourg. In Norway, German soldiers were urged to seduce women of 'Viking' blood, with the result that there were scores of *Lebensborn* children left to the mercy of the country's authorities after the war. Some were confined in mental asylums, because Norwegians feared they might contaminate Scandinavian blood through interracial relationships and raise a new generation of Nazi sympathizers.

Abduction

In all, 8,000 babies were delivered in *Lebensborn* clinics in Germany and 12,000 in Norway. But it wasn't enough for Himmler, who ordered the SS to abduct blond, blue-eyed children from their parents in the occupied territories and send them back for Aryanization by German foster families.

Folker Heinecke was a toddler when the advancing German army overran his parents' village in Crimea. He has no memories of his real parents and grew up with 'fanatical' Nazi foster parents whom he nevertheless learned to love. He eventually accepted that he was an orphan, but in his late sixties he was desperate to find the grave of his real parents so he could finally feel he had come home. He managed to identify them and the name of their village through documents held by a Red Cross Tracing centre. Folker said:

> I stood there and tried to imagine the SS advancing down here, their tanks and their motorbikes and their armoured cars, and I tried to imagine them taking a little boy who was guilty of nothing . . . I don't want to end up as many of the other children like me have, driven bitter and mad over what befell them. I just want to know who I was and what I might have been if things hadn't turned out the way they did. I have to keep searching to find something that might lead me to who my parents really were and where they are buried. Then I will have done my duty as a son. I will have honoured my real parents.

Salon Kitty

The Nazis advocated marriage, motherhood and fidelity, but they thought nothing of forcing German women to have sex with officers, prominent Party bosses and those suspected of disloyalty.

SS Gruppenführer Reinhard Heydrich, head of the Reich Main Security Office which controlled the Gestapo, the SS Intelligence Service and the Criminal Police, was not a man to make hasty decisions. Himmler's second in command liked to take his time, to consider the options, weighing up the merits of every case before committing himself. On his visits to Salon Kitty, he particularly enjoyed leafing through Madame Schmidt's photo album and choosing his girl for the evening. The ladies all had their particular attractions and had been trained to satisfy the most discerning customers, but the women who intrigued Heydrich the most were the high society ladies who had volunteered to serve the Fatherland in a most unusual capacity. What motivated them? The thrill of an illicit liaison? The opportunity to lead a secret life? Or was it the excitement of avoiding discovery that made the risk worth taking, like the thief who thinks himself too clever to be caught? It certainly couldn't be the money, for they were all affluent or married to men of means. And ardent Nazi though he was, Himmler's trusted lieutenant could not imagine they would have offered themselves out of National Socialist zeal.

Such thoughts were dispelled with the arrival of the girl. He had chosen well, he thought. And there would be other evenings. There was no hurry.

Madame Kitty ran a first class establishment on the third floor at number 11 Giesebrechtstrasse in Charlottenburg, a wealthy district of Berlin. The apartments had been refurbished to the highest standard, but unknown to its clientele there were new features behind the elegant façade. The walls had been fitted with concealed microphones which relayed every whisper and unguarded conversation to wax disc recording devices in the basement, which were manned by Gestapo agents.

It had been Heydrich's idea. In 1939 he had been entrusted by Himmler with tracing the source of high level leaks that threatened to give Germany's enemies warning of the attacks on Belgium, France and the Netherlands that were planned for the following spring. If the enemy had even the faintest suspicion of the blitzkrieg that was to be launched through the Ardennes they might divert enough troops to thwart the attack. But how to identify which high-ranking army officers and diplomats couldn't be trusted to keep the secret? The problem was given over to SS-Obersturmführer Walter Schellenberg, chief of the SD, the Reich Intelligence Service.

Schellenberg was something of a prude by all accounts, but he knew that the one thing that would loosen men's tongues was the prospect of impressing an attractive woman and there was no better opportunity to eavesdrop than in the bedroom of a brothel, one that would be closely monitored by the SD and operated by prostitutes trained to steer the conversation in the desired direction and draw out significant details. And after hostilities had broken out it would be prudent to monitor the political allegiances of prominent businessmen and military officers, to ensure their loyalty could be relied upon.

The original idea had been to secretly install a few bugging devices in a brothel that was known to attract diplomats and military personnel and trust to luck. However, shortly after Schellenberg had been given the task he was informed that the owner of the most prestigious establishment of that sort in Berlin was taking early retirement and might be persuaded to reopen her doors in return for her life.

Recalled from retirement

Kitty Schmidt had amassed a small fortune and had managed to smuggle most of it abroad, where it was accruing interest in a British bank account. But she had been under surveillance by the Gestapo and on 28 June she was arrested at the German/Dutch border and driven back to Gestapo headquarters in Berlin. There she was interrogated by Schellenberg himself and presented with damning evidence of her currency smuggling and use of false documents, all of which carried lengthy prison sentences. But she could spare herself the trouble if she agreed to co-operate. She had no choice but to agree. Her Berlin apartments would be renovated to allow the installation of the bugging devices and film cameras and 20 new girls would be employed, handpicked by Berlin's vice squad under the direction of Untersturmführer Karl Schwarz. While builders tore down the interior walls and bricked off the basement in Giesebrechtstrasse, the police raided night clubs and brothels throughout the city, bringing in more than a thousand girls to be questioned

THE POLICE RAIDED NIGHT CLUBS AND BROTHELS THROUGHOUT THE CITY, BRINGING IN MORE THAN A THOUSAND GIRLS TO BE QUESTIONED

by a team of academics and psychiatrists, who helped eliminate those they considered 'emotionally unreliable'.

After seven days of intense interviews all but 20 were rejected. These were then taken to Ordensburg, the officer's academy at Sonthofen in the Bavarian Alps, where they spent almost two months learning foreign languages, the use of codes, identifying military insignia, brushing up on current affairs and discovering how to elicit information without arousing suspicion.

By March Salon Kitty was open for business. Madame Schmidt had been told to keep her regular girls for existing customers and only to show the photo album to those clients who used the code, 'I come from Rothenburg'. These clients would be provided with chilled champagne and other refreshments while they waited ten minutes for the girl to arrive.

In the first year of business an estimated 10,000 men took advantage of Salon Kitty's services with 3,000 recordings made, of which the most damning was that made by Mussolini's son-in-law, Count Galeazzo, in which the count joked about how he and Il Duce ridiculed Hitler in private. Of more strategic significance was the night Nazi Foreign Minister Joachim von Ribbentrop invited his Spanish counterpart Don Ramón Serrano

Súñer to Giesebrechtstrasse. Súñer let slip his country's intentions to occupy Gibraltar, which the Germans were able to block just in time, because the Rock was needed to secure their supply routes to North Africa.

Britain joins the party

The Germans didn't have it all their own way though. In the winter of 1940 the brothel was under surveillance by a British agent by the name of Roger Wilson, who was posing as a junior press secretary at the Romanian Embassy. Salon Kitty was an open secret and the British were racking their brains as to how they might gain access and bug the building themselves when Wilson became suspicious of a group of workmen who were laying a multi-core cable outside the brothel. All of the men were wearing brand new overalls and acting as undercover agents do when they are trying to appear inconspicuous. Wilson took a chance and strolled across the street to take a closer look. It appeared that the men were routing an extension to SD headquarters, which confirmed that the building had been bugged. All the British would have to do to siphon off the information would be to get one of their technical experts into the building and attach taps to the interior wiring.

Wilson had a job convincing London to bankroll his nocturnal visits to a high-class brothel, but the investment paid dividends and for the next three years the British Secret Service benefited from the Nazi plan as much as the SD. There was only one high-ranking Nazi neither side were able to record. Every time Reinhard Heydrich made one of his 'inspection tours' the microphones were turned off.

Then in July 1942 an Allied bomb demolished the upper floors and the clients stopped coming. When Madame Kitty reopened on the ground floor those who braved the Allied air raids were of little interest to the

SD and they eventually handed the house back to her with the warning that if she breathed a word of what had occurred there she would not live to see the end of the war.

Kitty kept her word, dying in 1954 at the age of 71 without betraying the confidence of her clients. The whereabouts of the 25,000 discs recorded in the basement at number 11 Giesebrechtstrasse were never discovered. Author Peter Norden claimed to have seen them in a storeroom at the headquarters of the East German security services during his research for a book on the brothel, but if any have survived they are not revealing their secrets to anyone.

CHAPTER FIVE

Power of the Big Screen

The Nazis used film to indoctrinate the masses, while Goebbels indulged his passion for female stars . . .

No regime used imagery as effectively as the Nazis. Although Hitler possessed a remarkable gift for oratory, he understood that the most direct method of reaching the masses was through the use of simple symbols and strong iconic imagery. Both Albert Speer, who stage-managed the Nuremberg rallies, and Josef Goebbels, who presided over the Propaganda Ministry, knew that powerful images could make an indelible impression on the subconscious, stirring primitive emotions and awakening archetypal aspects of the psyche. Goebbels had been convinced of this after speaking with the German film-maker Fritz Hippler, who acted as his assistant and later directed the notorious and inflammatory propaganda feature *The Eternal Jew* (1940). Hippler believed that visuals were always more powerful than a verbal argument, which depends so much for its impact on the personality of the speaker, and he compared the cinema screen to a mirror in which the masses would see Germany, especially the poorer classes for whom film was the one form of culture they could afford.

Goebbels agreed. Rational thought was for intellectuals and required patience, insight and a receptive mind. The masses were more easily won over by appealing directly to their emotions and basest instincts.

But while the theatrical pomp and pageantry of the annual rallies incited the faithful to get in step behind the leadership and propaganda posters proclaimed National Socialist slogans to the general population, captive audiences in the dark, reverent hush of Germany's Kino theatres were subjected to a more subtle form of indoctrination.

Visual appeal

Goebbels had exploited the power of radio in the 1920s, broadcasting Nazi propaganda to great effect, but the potential of cinema to influence the civilian population had not yet been fully utilized. German films had made a considerable impact at home and abroad during the silent era, when the expressionist classic *The Cabinet of Dr Caligari* (1920), the early science fiction epic *Metropolis* (1927) and G. W. Pabst's social realist drama *Pandora's Box* (1929) captivated audiences with their contrasting visual styles, but Goebbels was no patron of the arts. Though he was a doctor of literature and philosophy and the author of several unpublished novels, he saw art primarily as a medium for distributing a political message and communicating a shared vision, rather than as a form of self-expression.

> **GOEBBELS HAD EXPLOITED THE POWER OF RADIO, BUT THE POTENTIAL OF CINEMA TO INFLUENCE THE CIVILIAN POPULATION HAD NOT YET BEEN UTILIZED**

Taking over Ufa

As soon as he had made himself comfortable behind his desk in the Ministry of Public Enlightenment and Propaganda in January 1933 and successfully fended off a rival bid for control of German cinema by Alfred Rosenberg's Front For German Culture, Goebbels embarked on a programme of indoctrination through print media, the fine arts, state-sponsored leisure activities, music, theatre and cinema. In late April he made an official visit to the Ufa (Universum Film AG) studios in Neubabelsburg, west of Berlin, to reassure management and production staff that German film was in good hands, but that 'alignment' with Nazi policy was required if those employed in the industry wanted to continue in their present posts. Film would have to be 'a champion of German culture' and not shallow entertainment copying the degenerate art of Hollywood – which had a hidden agenda to corrupt Aryan society because the American studios were run by Jews and their films featured coloured actors and decadent Negro jazz music. Kitsch and inferior art would not be tolerated.

The principal German studio, Ufa had just been hit by a substantial loss in revenue due to a blanket boycott of German films by Britain and America and could not afford to lose state sponsorship. So they accepted the inevitable and agreed to submit all films to the new Reich Film Board for approval. In return for their co-operation the Nazis established a new source of funding, the Film Credit Bank, with the pledge of 10 million marks towards new productions. Although the main shareholders were legitimate financial institutions (the Dresden Bank, the Deutsche Bank, the Commercial and Private Bank as well as the government's Reichs Kredit-Gesellschaft), the money was effectively under Goebbels' personal control as he decided which projects would receive state funding (typically between 50 and 70 per cent of their production costs).

Goebbels had become a despot in his own domain but saw himself in the role of an orchestral conductor, co-ordinating the efforts of many talented individuals hired to perform a chosen piece under the guidance of his baton. He would choose the programme, audition the performers and dictate the tempo. But he would not be satisfied with issuing guidelines and directives. After each film was completed he would have a private screening and invariably demanded changes to comply with Nazi policy.

Film buff

But Goebbels had a genuine passion for movies; he watched at least one every day even during the war. Although he steeled himself to watch every type of film so that he could learn something from even the most mediocre potboiler, he had a personal dislike for crime and American screwball comedy and considered rustic dramas to be 'vulgar'. According to director Arthur Rabenalt, Goebbels' favourite movies were *Gone With The Wind* (1939), *Ben Hur* (1925) and Disney's *Snow White and the Seven Dwarfs* (1937), although he also derived great pleasure from two of the musicals he had helped put into production – *Es leuchten die Sterne* ('The Stars Are Shining', 1937) and *Patrioten* ('The Patriots', 1936) – which were seen by between 15 and 25 million people and proved highly profitable.

Goebbels understood that audiences didn't go to the cinema to be educated but to be entertained. Nazi cinema would out-glamourize Hollywood. Its stars would shine brighter than those of MGM, Warner Brothers and Fox. He, Josef Goebbels, would wield more power than the studio moguls in America and he would enjoy the company of the most beautiful women in the Reich, stars such as Olga Tschechowa, Marika Rökk, Zarah Leander and Kristina Söderbaum who, he imagined, would be grateful for the celebrity status his patronage would guarantee. How grateful they would be, only time would tell.

Zarah Leander

The Nazis had prohibited Jews from working in the film industry and banned the screening of films that had been made by Jewish directors before Hitler assumed power. But after Marlene Dietrich left Germany for Hollywood there were few female stars of a similar magnitude to take

THOUGH SHE HAD CRITICIZED THE NAZI REGIME, GOEBBELS CONTINUED TO MAKE OVERTURES TO DIETRICH TO RETURN AND STAR IN GERMAN FILMS

her place. Curiously, though she had emigrated to America in 1930 and had publicly criticized the Nazi regime, Goebbels continued to make overtures to Dietrich to return and star in German films. As late as November 1937 he noted that she would not be free from her Paramount contract until the following year, but that she 'remained committed to Germany'.

The four actresses who possessed even a glimmer of Dietrich's charisma were foreigners and one, Zarah Leander (1907–1981), was known to have Jewish grand-parents. Goebbels was deeply suspicious of her for this reason, while her insistence on being paid two-thirds of her salary in Danish krone was a constant irritant to him, as was her repeated refusal to apply for German citizenship.

At a private party he reputedly asked her outright if she was Jewish. 'Zarah – that's a Jewish name, isn't it?' he inquired, to which she replied, 'Well, what about Josef?' But Hitler held her in the highest regard and would hear nothing said against her.

Leander was a statuesque Swede with a smoky voice enhanced by a continuous supply of cigarettes and a taste for a Scandinavian liquor known as Aquavit. It was rumoured that the composer Franz Lehár was forced to transpose her arias down two octaves when she starred in his operetta *The Merry Widow* in Stockholm in 1931 and that she was bombarded with fan mail addressed to 'Herr Leander' from those who had only heard her records. But when she made the transition from stage to screen there could be no doubting her gender.

A 1938 issue of *Filmwelt* announced the arrival of a new screen goddess:

> This incredibly impeccable and sculptured face mirrors everything that moves a woman: wistfulness and pain, love and bliss, melancholy and resignation. In her attitude as an actress, Zarah Leander is the epitome of 'spiritualized sensuality'. As dark as her low, undefinable alto – which is able to represent so excitingly the expression of hidden female desires – is also her essence.

Her luminous Nordic beauty and heavy accent drew comparisons with Garbo and though Goebbels confided to his diary that he thought her 'very overrated', she was popular with German audiences who flocked to see her in a series of erotically charged films beginning with *Zu neuen Ufern* ('To New Shores', 1937), which made her the highest paid female actress in Nazi Germany. Her final Ufa contract guaranteed her half a million Reichsmarks for three pictures, which she invested in a fish cannery in her native country as if anticipating her return if the Nazis lost the war.

She was given roles that emphasized her smouldering sensuality and suggestive songs such as 'Can Love Be A Sin?', which added to her allure. These were specially written for her by her favourite songwriter Bruno Balz, whom she defended when he was arrested by the Gestapo for 'immoral acts' with a Hitler Youth member in 1942. It was the only time Goebbels came to her aid, because he too wanted to spare Balz from public humiliation and a jail sentence. The songwriter was too valuable to morale.

Otherwise, Leander declared herself neutral, admitting that she was a 'political idiot', although recently declassified documents from the Swedish Secret Service suggest that she might have been a Soviet spy.

Gay icon?

Leander's height proved a problem during the making of her most celebrated film *The Great Love* (1942). According to her co-star Wolfgang Preiss, the producers couldn't find women who were sufficiently tall to form a chorus line during a dance number. Then someone had the bright idea of using men. But where would they find enough men of the right height and build who would be willing to be dressed in women's clothes? In one of the most bizarre episodes in the history of the Third Reich, members of the SS were drafted in to don wigs, women's costumes and make-up and everyone on the set was sworn to secrecy on pain of death. But the deception is all too obvious if viewed in close-up, where the men's stubble is clearly visible. Even if it had not been for this episode, Leander's androgynous, high camp act would have ensured she became a gay icon.

After her Berlin home was bombed by the Allies in 1943, she returned to Sweden to the consternation of her German fans and condemnation from Goebbels, who banned her films and accused her of being a traitor to the Reich.

Kristina Söderbaum

There was no mistaking Kristina Söderbaum (1912–2001) for a man in drag. The curvaceous Swedish blonde starred in ten box-office hits in Nazi Germany, all directed by her possessive husband Veit Harlan, who became known for directing the most bombastic, expensive and colourful films of the period as well as the most notorious, *Jud Süss*. But more remarkably, she enjoyed stardom during the Third Reich without having to submit to Goebbels' obsequious charm. It might have been that the diminutive, club-footed Goebbels did not fancy having to face down Harlan, who was fearless when it came to defending his wife from overzealous admirers. Or perhaps the Propaganda Minister could not afford to make an enemy of one of the few loyal Nazi directors left in Germany at the time.

Harlan cast his new wife in brooding melodramas in

which she frequently played the tragic heroine who sacrifices her honour and then herself to save her man. She was deflowered and drowned so often that she was dubbed *Reichswasserleiche* ('the Empire's water corpse'). Her corn-coloured hair and porcelain skin were lit to emphasize her fragility and from 1941 all of her films were photographed in luxurious Agfacolor, which brought out the bloom in her china doll complexion.

Her most popular films were those which pandered to the Nazi creed, although she also made innocuous romantic movies such as *Verwehte Spuren* (1938), later remade as *So Long At The Fair* (1950), with Dirk Bogarde, and *Die Reise nach Tilsit* (1938), which was itself a remake of F. W. Murnau's *Sunrise* (1927). The latter became a cause célèbre after Magda Goebbels walked out of the premiere when she thought she recognized a veiled reference to her husband's affair with the Czech actress Lída Baarová.

But it was *Jud Süss* (1940) that brought the couple before a Nazi war crimes court after the war, on charges that the film had contributed to the Holocaust. It had been shown in almost every major city in occupied Europe shortly before the round-up and transportation of Jews to the death camps, in order to encourage the mute co-operation of the civilian population. Both were cleared but their careers were over. Söderbaum turned to the theatre in a play written by her husband and was vilified by former fans, some of whom threatened to murder them both. She made a few inferior German films in the 1950s, then earned a modest living as a professional photographer.

Olga Tschechowa

No less glamorous was Olga Tschechowa, who was born in Russia but of German stock. A star of the Soviet stage and the former wife of Mikhail Chekhov, nephew of the famous playwright, she emigrated to Berlin in 1920. At Ufa she worked with F. W. Murnau and later featured in films directed by René Clair and Alfred Hitchcock. But her greatest performance came when she cast herself as a friend to Adolf Hitler, while acting, allegedly, as a Soviet spy.

Unknown to the Nazis, she had received her travel papers in exchange for future services. However, little was required of her until Hitler came to power, but then her Soviet paymasters were impatient to learn what the German leader planned as his country stepped up its rearmament programme and demanded the return of territories to the east.

By the early 1930s Olga had made the successful transition from silent movies to talkies and was one of the biggest box-office draws in Germany, starring in such films as *Der Choral von Leuthen* (1933), a historical pageant celebrating the life of Frederick the Great.

Hitler was an admirer and when he invited her to dine alone with him in Berlin she saw the opportunity to repay her debt.

When photographs of her cosying up to the dictator at a reception appeared in the Russian press she was accused of being a traitor to her country, but behind closed doors she intervened to save the life of her brother, a Soviet assassin who had been sent to Germany to kill Hitler. He was languishing in a concentration camp after the plot had been uncovered and was certain to be executed, but Olga used all her feminine wiles to secure his release. Her intervention, however, brought her to the attention of Heinrich Himmler, head of the SS and the Gestapo, who ordered an investigation into her off-screen activities. But the star had her spies in the regime and when news of her imminent arrest reached her, she had a surprise for Himmler. The Reichsführer burst into her apartment and found Olga had company – Hitler himself was being entertained. He ordered Himmler to leave at once.

From that moment on Olga Tschechowa was assured

of Hitler's protection. She continued to star in German films and enjoyed her celebrity and the patronage of the Nazi elite. After the war she was summoned back to Moscow where Stalin received her in private. What passed between them is not known, but she was then free to return to Germany and resume her career until the 1970s. She died in Munich in 1980, aged 95.

Marika Rökk

Musical comedy actress, singer and dancer Marika Rökk (1913–2004) was already an international star of musical revue when the Nazis stormed to power in 1933. But the Egyptian-born beauty of Hungarian parentage had yet to make a movie. Her first German feature set the pattern for a series of escapist entertainments in which she styled herself as the German Ginger Rogers, an ever-cheerful sprite who danced, sang and laughed her way across the screen all through the war years to the delight of cinemagoers. These upbeat morale-boosting movies were appreciated all the more when the bombs were falling and defeat seemed inevitable. Her German debut *Light Cavalry* in 1935 was quickly followed by several variations on the same formula and in 1940 she received lavish praise and a large bouquet of flowers for her dual role in *Kora Terry* from a grateful Führer, who appreciated the diversion from the serious business of subjugating Europe. She acknowledged the gesture in a gushing telegram.

> **A GRATEFUL FÜHRER APPRECIATED THE DIVERSION FROM THE SERIOUS BUSINESS OF SUBJUGATING EUROPE**

'If I somewhat diverted you, mein Führer, for a few brief moments from the burden of your important responsibilities, I shall be forever proud and happy. With a German salute, your Marika Rökk.'

After the war she was shocked to be banned from

performing for three years, having been in frivolous musical comedies, but she was soon back in favour with the Allied occupying forces, who were also in need of cheering up, and with the Austrians, who had not lost their taste for frothy, saccharine-sweet sentimental songs and girls with a permanent smile on their faces.

Lilian Harvey

Of the quartet of 1930s German starlets who put their best foot forward during the Third Reich only Lilian Harvey (1906–1968) satisfied the Nazis' racial requirements – and she was half English.

Born Helene Pape in north London to a British mother and a German father, Lilian was sent to live with an aunt in Switzerland when the Great War broke out. From there she studied at the Berlin State Opera School of Dance and on graduating found her way into pictures in the early 1920s. Her singing and dancing abilities and facility with languages made her an asset in 'talkies' and specifically in a series of 11 operettas she made at Ufa with screen partner Willy Fritsch. It was routine to film the same story in three languages, using the same sets but with a rotating cast. Harvey, however, was able to demand three times her co-stars' salaries by virtue of her fluency in German, English and French.

Laurence Olivier made his screen debut starring opposite Lilian in the English version of *Hokuspokus*. Her most celebrated film *The Congress Dances* (1931) brought offers from Hollywood, but after four poorly performing films for 20th Century Fox she returned to Germany to be reunited with director and lover Paul Martin. Had she stayed to star in *George White's Scandals* she might have become a major star in America, because it made a name for her replacement, Alice Faye.

Her girlish, feather-brained personality was summed up by the anonymous reviewer of *My Lips Betray* (1933):

'A likeable and occasionally lyric comedienne, her efforts to enliven a heavy-handed and humourless script result in a performance stuffed with that particular form of girlish charm which drives strong men to dipsomania and homicide.'

But though she affected a girlish personality on screen she appears to have been made of very much sterner material in reality.

After she found herself under contract to Josef Goebbels, who made it clear that he would not tolerate her friendships with several Jewish colleagues who had been deprived of their positions, she defied him and was subsequently warned off by the Gestapo. In 1937 she put up bail for Jewish choreographer and friend Jens Keith, who was being charged under Paragraph 175 of the German Criminal Code, which criminalized homosexuality. With her agreement he fled to France and she was arrested and threatened with imprisonment for having aided a fugitive. Fearing for her life, she escaped first to France and then to England, abandoning a considerable fortune that she had amassed through her earnings in the movies. Her property was confiscated and her bank accounts were seized, leaving her with nothing but the jewels she was wearing when she arrived in England. Fortunately they were real emeralds and diamonds valued at almost £60,000.

Runaway director

When Goebbels visited the vast and rambling Ufa film studios in Babelsberg, west of Berlin, during his first year in office he must have felt the same as Orson Welles when given complete control of his first project, *Citizen Kane* (1941). The studio was indeed the 'biggest electric train set a boy ever had', only Goebbels also had casting couch privileges and intended to use them. Goebbels, who favoured dark-eyed brunettes, naturally assumed that the leading German filmmakers and their stars would consider it an honour to work for the Reich and he summoned them one by one to the Chancellery for a personal interview, but they were not all as grateful as the Nazis expected.

Fritz Lang admitted that he was flattered to hear that Hitler was a big admirer of *Metropolis* (1927) and also of *Die Nibelungen* (1924), which had brought the Führer to tears, and was pleased to hear that Hitler had said of him, 'Here is a man who will give us great Nazi films.' But Lang wisely asked for time to consider such an important proposal and used it to arrange safe passage to America. His absence forced the Nazis to turn to their stock journeymen directors like Karl Ritter, although they were more than fortunate in having documentary film-maker Leni Riefenstahl to helm two of the most memorable and visually impressive records of the Nazi years: *Triumph of the Will* (1935) and *Olympia* (1938).

Leni Riefenstahl

Leni Riefenstahl (born Helene Bertha Amalie in 1902) had starred in a series of critically acclaimed and commercially successful 'mountain films' (Bergfilms) for director Arnold Fanck during the late 1920s, which included *The White Hell of Pitz Palu* (1929). She did her own climbing (famously in bare feet for one scene) and performed her own stunts, which included being swept away in an avalanche and emerging unscathed. Dubbed 'Hitler's pin-up girl', she was admired for her indomitable courage and chiselled Nordic features. But she became fascinated by the art of filmmaking and withdrew from acting to work behind the camera. (It is possible that she abandoned acting after failing to secure the leading role in von Sternberg's *The Blue Angel* (1930), which went to her rival, Marlene Dietrich.)

Fanck taught her how to combine unusual camera

angles, coloured filters, diffused lighting, lenses and different film stock to determine the look and emotional impact of a film and he showed her how editing could heighten tension and bring drama to a scene.

Riefenstahl was inspired: 'The editing room became a magic workshop for me'.

Victory of Faith

Her first feature, *The Blue Light* (1932), earned her international recognition after it was awarded the Silver Medal at the Venice Film festival that year, for which Hitler honoured her with an invitation to the Chancellery and an offer to document the 1933 Party rally in Nuremberg.

As a devoted admirer of the man she believed would make Germany the envy of Europe, she felt privileged and more than capable of presenting the Party in all its military glory. In 1937 she would tell the *Detroit News*: 'Hitler is the greatest man who ever lived. He truly is without fault, so simple and at the same time possessed of masculine strength.'

A year before her death in 2003 she told *Die Welt* that the first projects Hitler offered her were crude propaganda features, *SA-Mann Brand* and *Hitler Youth Quex*, which were later given to other directors. She claimed to have turned them down, which made Hitler angry. Then he suggested she made a film on the history of the Party, which she also rejected. But when he asked her to document the 1933 Nuremberg Rally she agreed. She couldn't afford to miss out on the opportunity to align herself with the leader whose presence would guarantee the film worldwide distribution and earn her enormous publicity. Hitler ordered Goebbels to put the resources of the Reich Film Board at her disposal, but he did nothing, presumably in the hope that the Führer would forget about it.

By that time Goebbels, for many reasons, already hated me and he did not follow Hitler's direction. As a result there was a big argument between Goebbels and Hitler . . . he called Dr. Goebbels and chewed him out in my presence. I almost sank into the floor, it was frightening. Because Hitler wanted me to come out on top against Goebbels, his aversion to me was increased.

But even with Hitler's endorsement, Riefenstahl experienced resentment from the male-dominated film industry and the Party simply because she was a woman. 'The Party attempted to boycott the project. In Nuremberg I received neither film supplies nor money, simply nothing at all.'

She then befriended Albert Speer. He found her a good cameraman, Walter Frentz, who brought two experienced assistants with him. According to Riefenstahl, though, they were Nazi hirelings who attempted to sabotage the film: 'Party people knocked over the cameras and a lot was destroyed.' She complained to Speer who advised her to inform Hitler. 'But then I'll have even more enemies,' she said, to which he replied, 'You must tell him everything.'

Soon afterwards, a low-level Party employee rented a tiny room for her to edit the film in, which was an out-of-service elevator. It was a blatant attempt to show what he and his colleagues thought of her. An old cutting table was installed and a female assistant was ordered to help her.

But after all her efforts Hitler refused to approve the film's release. Riefenstahl said that Goebbels had it destroyed because every shot of Hitler included Ernst Roehm, the SA leader who had been murdered on Hitler's orders by the time *Victory of Faith* was ready for release. In comparison with her subsequent films it was flat and rather clumsy, so the claim that it was shelved because it included shots of Roehm might have been a face-saving excuse.

Triumph of the Will

Uncharacteristically, Hitler gave the director a second chance the following year and this time she planned her shots as meticulously as Speer was to stage-manage the event itself.

> During the preparations I walked around Nuremberg with the camera people, especially with Sepp Allgeier, who was the most important to me, and determined the camera positions with him and how we would cinematically dramatize the crowds.

In order to divert the audience from the static nature of the speeches, she had the idea of setting up a track around the speaker, ensuring audience interest by keeping the camera moving even when the subject was still.

> I didn't stage a single scene, but rather I simply picked up with the camera what there was to see in the arena. It's also been written that I had who knows how many cameramen for the film, when in reality I had only thirteen and of these only two or three that were very good, the best being Allgeier. The rest were students. The quality of the film was determined on the cutting table and by the background music.

Her own assessment of *Triumph of the Will* was that it was 'primitive and simple', but that it was helped immensely by the addition of Herbert Windt's music. Although it is evident that several key sequences of *Triumph of the Will* (1935) were restaged for the cameras, the result is a visually impressive example of film as propaganda, though repulsive in its veneration of the fascist military mindset and its deification of Hitler.

At the premiere Hitler proclaimed it to be 'a totally unique and incomparable glorification of the power and beauty of our movement' and Riefenstahl to be the embodiment of the 'perfect German woman'. The following year she marshalled her forces and considerable energies to document the 1936 Berlin Olympics, with unlimited access and resources provided by Goebbels' Propaganda Ministry.

Documenting the Olympics

'I had the desire to make the Olympic idea visible in the film – from its roots to the present.' This she achieved by filming the athletes as if they were living works of art – a theme introduced in the opening sequence as classical statues come to life through a series of dissolves – and by lighting them to heighten the muscle structure and the body beautiful in slow motion. 'Goebbels himself chose me for the Olympia film – even though he was against me as a woman – he had high regard for me as an artist,' recalled Riefenstahl.

GOEBBELS WAS 'VERY ANNOYED' TO SEE FOOTAGE OF THE BLACK RUNNER JESSE OWENS INCLUDED

But Goebbels was 'very annoyed' to see footage of the black runner Jesse Owens included and demanded that the French distributor cut him out of the film. It is said that the distributor would only agree to this if the sequences showing Hitler were excised too.

With its innovative use of multiple-camera set-ups, slow motion sequences, crane shots, rhythmic montages and smooth tracking shots, *Olympia* (1938) raised the modern documentary to an art form and established the standard by which all subsequent documentaries would be measured. It had taken 18 months to edit the thousands of feet of footage and it would be acknowledged as a considerable technical achievement. But although the film was showered with international accolades, its director was shunned by the American movie community.

Boycotted by the studios

During a promotional visit to America in November 1938 all but two of the Hollywood studios refused to receive Riefenstahl on their lots, the exceptions being silent comedy producer Hal Roach and Walt Disney. When informed that the Jewish studio moguls had refused to meet her because of the events of *Kristallnacht* earlier that week, she told her US agent that she would stay in her hotel room until 'this damn Jewish thing is no longer in the headlines'.

Her repeated claim that 'Work and peace are the only messages of *Triumph of the Will*' was revealed to be fallacious when German troops marched into Prague five months later, in March 1939. However, she remained stubbornly contemptuous of her critics, who saw her as a cynical opportunist who possessed an unerring eye and a sense for visual poetry but a blind spot for the nature of the regime that she served.

'I've never done anything I didn't want to, and nothing I've been ashamed of,' she said in response to accusations that she could have followed Billy Wilder, Fritz Lang and the other filmmakers to America.

In retrospect she claimed to have been 'appalled' to discover what atrocities the Nazis had committed and to have viewed her documentaries in a different light. 'As it later became known what terrible things happened in his name and his Party one was appalled, very deeply and rightfully appalled.' But she insisted that during the time she had been 'Hitler's favourite filmmaker' she had 'never thought about politics'.

And yet, when France fell she wrote to Hitler, expressing her unbounded admiration.

With indescribable joy, deeply moved and filled with burning gratitude, we share with you, my Führer, your and Germany's greatest victory, the entry of

German troops into Paris. You exceed anything human imagination has the power to conceive, achieving deeds without parallel in the history of mankind. How can we ever thank you?

Loyal Hitler supporter

Riefenstahl remained a loyal and enthusiastic supporter of Hitler until her death at the age of 101. In 1939 she served as a frontline correspondent in Poland, where she witnessed the massacre of civilians in Końskie. Despite claiming to have been horrified at the executions, she filmed Hitler's triumphant entry into Warsaw just weeks later. She was subsequently accused of promising Romany labour camp prisoners their freedom in return for acting as extras in an unfinished film, *Tiefland*. All were later gassed at Auschwitz, according to fellow inmates, though Riefenstahl claimed: 'Nothing happened to any of them,' a statement she was subsequently forced to retract.

Riefenstahl had demonstrated physical courage during her days as a star of Fanck's 'Alpine films', but she was morally spineless and complicit in glorifying a murderous regime. She admitted that in the beginning she was 'very impressed' by Hitler, particularly the way he had reversed unemployment, but that in 1937 she was shocked to hear him condemn Goya and van Gogh as 'degenerate' during the opening of an exhibition in Munich. If he could make such misjudgements on art, she thought, what might he be capable of with regard to politics?

Goebbels was in awe of Riefenstahl's talent, describing her in his diary as 'the only star who understands us' and commending her National Socialist zeal, but he harboured a personal animosity towards her because she commanded Hitler's rapt attention. Riefenstahl subsequently denied that she was a die-hard Nazi, a claim contradicted by her correspondence with the notorious Julius Streicher, in which she begged for his help in the avoidance of making royalty payments to the Jewish screenwriter of *The Blue Light*. She also removed his name and that of her Jewish producer so that the film could qualify as *judenfrei* (free of Jews) and be reissued in 1938.

Post-war pariah

After the war she was treated as a pariah by the film community both in Germany and abroad.

> I was made out to be a monster, maybe because I was a woman, or perhaps because I had made more famous films, so that envious persons came on the scene. The newspapers wrote, 'Should we let her live?' or, 'Shouldn't she be on trial in Nuremberg too?' I was suddenly slandered as a super-Nazi, as a leader who, like Joan of Arc carrying the flag, marched the troops to victory at Orléans . . . it was simply jealousy and blind hatred. Others wanted to de-Nazify themselves by attacking me. By doing that they wanted to say, 'I'm not like Riefenstahl, she really was a fanatical National Socialist.'

Goebbels lavished praise on *Triumph of the Will*, which he preferred to overtly political feature films such as *Hitlerjunge Quex* ('Hitler Youth Quest', 1933) and *Hans Westmar* (1934), as they paled in comparison to the grandeur and choreographed parade of military might on display in Riefenstahl's documentaries.

Hitler's last film appearance

Although *Triumph of the Will* was a great success in Germany and attracted critical acclaim for its aesthetic qualities (and condemnation for its political content), Goebbels advised Hitler not to make any further appearances on film. He did not want to risk over-exposing his 'star', so he ensured that he only figured briefly in newsreels. Instead, historical dramas such as *The Great King* (1942), which depicted the life of Frederick the Great, were used to substitute a historical figure for the Führer, whose benign leadership was seen as a parallel to the present.

Goebbels had seen the impact Eisenstein's *Battleship Potemkin* had made on audiences and wanted the Nazi heroes and heroines in German films to arouse equally strong reactions and feelings. But he knew that if he commissioned nothing but patriotic militarist pictures the audience would quickly tire of them and seek entertainment elsewhere, so he shrewdly balanced historical epics with frivolous musical comedies and emotive melodramas. These would appeal to all audiences and stave off their desire to see foreign movies, which had been banned in Germany. During the Third Reich 90 per cent of the films produced and approved by the Propaganda Ministry had no overt political content.

Boosting flagging morale

After the defeat at Stalingrad in 1943, Nazi cinema concentrated on morale-boosting subjects exemplified by *Münchausen* (1943), the beautifully shot escapist fantasy chronicling the far-fetched 18th century adventures of Baron Hieronymus von Münchausen. Goebbels' pet project, the film was designed to rival Hollywood, celebrate the 25th anniversary of the Ufa studios and denigrate the inhabitants of the countries visited by the fictional Münchausen. The master spin doctor made the most of his ministerial authority, earning the nickname 'the Ram' through his amorous exploits on the casting couch. But by the following year, when the Allies invaded Fortress Europe, even he could see that his days of luxury and sexual conquest were numbered.

The last production he supervised was a thinly veiled allusion to Germany's impending doom. A metaphor for the critical situation, *Kolberg* (1945), a 19th century costume drama, dramatized the courageous last stand made by the inhabitants of a German town, who were besieged and eventually overrun by the armies of Napoleon. It featured 200,000 German troops drafted in from the Eastern Front and premiered just months before capitulation.

> ## THE LAST PRODUCTION HE SUPERVISED WAS A THINLY VEILED ALLUSION TO GERMANY'S IMPENDING DOOM

The strange affair of Dr Goebbels

The Nazi elite were as duplicitous and self-serving as any politicians, proving the old adage about absolute power corrupting those who possess it.

As Minister of Propaganda, Goebbels promoted race hatred, but carried on a secret affair with an 'inferior' Slav, Czech movie actress Lída Baarová. They met at a party the year before she found fame at the age of 20 with her first German starring role in *Barcarolle* (1935).

> He told me he loved me time and again and I felt his eyes burning into my back every time we were in the same room together . . . His voice seemed to go straight into me. I felt a light tingling in my back, as if his words were trying to stroke my body.

She eagerly accepted invitations to share intimate evenings aboard his yacht *Baldur*, but he seemed over-eager to impress her. He invited her to a Nazi Party rally where he was due to deliver a speech and promised to give her a secret sign to demonstrate his devotion. It alarmed her to think that she might be getting involved with someone who was so intense and possessive, but as she prepared to make a quiet exit a messenger arrived with a bouquet of roses and a framed photograph of her tenacious suitor. 'He was a master of the hunt, whom nobody and nothing could escape,' she recalled.

But to her surprise he proved a patient lover, content to have her company during weekend trips to his lodge on the shore of Lake Lanke outside Berlin and taking her on drives to the country in his chauffeur-driven limousine. He would call her for long talks on the telephone, adopting the alias Herr Muller, and would hang up if it was answered by her live-in lover and co-star, Gustav Fröhlich, who played Freder in Lang's *Metropolis*.

Eventually Goebbels couldn't contain his feelings any longer and after inviting her to the lodge he lit a log fire, drew her close and kissed her saying, 'Liduschka, I have never in my life been so inflamed with love for a woman.' He could be charming and amusing, she remembered, entertaining her with his accurate impressions of Hitler, but also cruel and vindictive such as when he rescinded Fröhlich's exemption from military service and had him sent to the Front, so he could be alone with Baarová. However, there was still Magda to contend with.

In the autumn of 1938, Goebbels called his mistress to inform her that he had confessed all to his wife and that Magda demanded a meeting to discuss the terms under which she might be prepared to allow the relationship to continue. According to Baarová, Magda told her, 'I am the mother of his children, I am only interested in this house in which we live. What happens outside does not concern me. But you must promise me one thing: you must not have a child by him.'

End of the romance

Goebbels bought both women expensive jewellery to seal the arrangement, but Magda later changed her mind and took her troubles to Hitler. Baarová claimed Goebbels was sobbing when he called the next morning to tell her that Hitler had refused to grant Magda a divorce and had threatened to remove him from his post and reassign him to Japan if he refused to break off the relationship. 'My wife is a devil,' he told her.

'Goebbels fell in love with me, but I didn't love him,' Baarová told the London *Times* many years later.

> I was afraid of him and what he would do because I kept turning down his offers, although he always behaved charmingly and was always very nice to me. I remember he once gave me a gold bracelet for Christmas. Hitler made a huge fuss about it. He called Goebbels in and told him to drop me and return to his wife and children. I couldn't take the pressure and I returned to Prague. Goebbels never tried to contact me again.

At the 1942 Venice film festival she found herself sitting uncomfortably close to her former lover, who publicly snubbed her. 'He must have recognized me, but he did not make a single movement. He was always the master of self-control.'

Desperate to win back Hitler's approval after being reconciled with his wife, Goebbels conceived *Kristallnacht* in November 1938, ostensibly as a 'spontaneous' reaction to the assassination of a German embassy official in Paris. In one night of violence 267 synagogues were burned to the ground, countless Jewish cemeteries were desecrated and 7,500 Jewish-owned businesses looted and their windows smashed, giving rise to the name *Kristallnacht* – 'Night of Broken Glass'.

Alone and penniless

Hitler was also smitten with the Czech actress after spotting her during a visit to the film studios in 1934. Whenever he noticed her at official functions he would stare at her unsmiling while appearing to be listening to another guest. Hitler enjoyed the company of glamorous young film stars and at the first opportunity he invited Baarová to tea at the Chancellery. She arrived at the wheel of her own Mercedes, which Hitler found rather daring. Her high spirits and supreme self-confidence reminded him of his 'beautiful and tragic' niece, which she took as a compliment until he told her that Geli had shot herself out of love for her 'Uncle Adolf'. Baarová became a regular guest at the Führer's intimate parties, but after she declined an offer to apply for German citizenship by saying that she had no desire to renounce her Czech nationality, she found herself frozen out of the Führer's inner circle.

When Hitler learned of her affair with his Propaganda Minister he ordered her expulsion from Berlin and banned her films from being screened. With his approval the Gestapo organized hecklers to shout abuse when she attended the premiere of her new film, *Der Spieler* ('The Player', 1938), and soon afterwards she left Germany, knowing that her life would have been made intolerable had she stayed.

From Prague she travelled to Italy in search of work, later finding parts in films by de Sica and Fellini, and then to Austria where she secured a small role in Rainer Werner Fassbinder's *The Bitter Tears of Petra von Kant* (1972). But accusations that she had been a Gestapo spy plagued her to the end of her days and the work soon dried up.

'There's no doubt that Goebbels was an interesting character,' she admitted in 1997, 'a charming and intelligent man and a very good storyteller. You could guarantee that he would keep a party going with his little asides and jokes.'

But he was entirely without principles. 'Thanks to him I fell into the depths of Hell.' But if she didn't regret the affair she certainly regretted her decision to remain in Germany when she could have accepted an offer to work in Hollywood. 'I could have been as famous as Marlene Dietrich,' she brooded, alone and penniless in her Salzburg apartment.

She had kept no souvenirs of the affair, having torn up every photograph she possessed of herself and Goebbels together. Her last wish was to return to her native country, but she remained in Austria until her death in 2000, believing she would not have been welcome in the country she felt she had betrayed.

CHAPTER SIX

The Nazi Elite

The Nazis told women what to wear and where to shop, but the leaders' wives flaunted the latest fashions and luxury goods

The role of German women in Nazi crimes was not seriously considered by historians until the late 1980s. Until then it was generally accepted that the majority of German women were as much victims of the regime as their civilian counterparts in the occupied territories and that the cruelty they suffered at the hands of the advancing Soviet troops was sufficient punishment for their initial support for Hitler, not to mention the privations they endured in the years immediately after the capitulation. After all, the men had done the killing while the women, with a few monstrous exceptions, had merely kept the home until it was bombed and shelled to rubble. The loss of their houses and apartments, their sons and sweethearts, fathers and friends, together with the carefree lifestyle they had enjoyed at the expense of others in Warsaw, Paris and other cities in the conquered countries was deemed fitting retribution. There was even grudging respect for the 'rubble women' of Berlin who cleared their capital brick by brick, even if they did lay the blame for such wanton destruction entirely on the Allies.

There might have been reluctance on the part of male historians (and they were predominantly male) to probe into the role of 'ordinary'

> **THE MEN HAD DONE THE KILLING WHILE THE WOMEN HAD MERELY KEPT THE HOME UNTIL IT WAS BOMBED AND SHELLED TO RUBBLE**

women on account of the brutality they had suffered at the hands of the Soviets. It was so much easier to categorize the majority of German women as mere 'fellow travellers', a group that was officially recognized by the de-Nazification courts as meriting condemnation rather than imprisonment.

It was only with the publication of Claudia Koonz's *Mothers in the Fatherland* (1987) that this deliberate 'oversight' was addressed and the role of women in the Third Reich reassessed. But admirable and thorough though Koonz had been, she limited her study to the secretaries and filing clerks who oiled the machinery of state and kept its meticulous records, while marginalizing the concentration camp guards and female staff at the euthanasia institutes as freakish aberrations and the wives of Nazi officers as frivolous socialites. Koonz identified the majority of the most fervent female Nazis as predominantly middle class and held all equally accountable.

A class apart

However, it is now clear that the Nazis created a new elite who considered themselves a class apart from the working women of Germany and distinct from the aristocracy. Moreover, they openly flaunted their privileges and indulged in the luxuries their male benefactors declared to be decadent and unbecoming of the master race. Like the wives and mistresses of the Roman emperors, these 20th century social climbers were privy to the crimes being perpetrated in their name and it was in their interest to preserve the impression of innocence.

High fashion and the classless national community that the Nazis wished to create (or the image of it) were mutually exclusive. Haute couture was for the upper class. It was an expensive habit to indulge in and it was time-consuming. Shop girls, schoolteachers, clerks and secretaries didn't have the time to browse at leisure through fashion magazines on a regular basis and invest in a wardrobe that would give them the choice of a dozen outfits and the shoes to match. They had no choice but to comply with the regime's edict to dress modestly, with functionality uppermost in their minds. The Nazi hierarchy became the new elite, the nouveau riche, who took it upon themselves to live a life of luxury and leisure under the pretence of setting the standards for their inferiors to follow.

Dress rules for the Hausfrau

At first Nazi propaganda appealed to women's patriotic duty, urging the loyal Hausfrau to buy only what was essential and functional and to purchase these goods from German stores, avoiding department stores such as Tietz, a chain owned by Jews. When Hitler came to power, these particular shops were 'Aryanized' and renamed 'Hertie'.

On 1 April 1933 the Nazis organized a national boycott of Jewish businesses, during which brown-shirted SA thugs painted the Star of David on shop windows and intimidated customers. But it would be impossible to man the streets in such numbers every day, so the Party called on women to avoid Jewish stores in the hope that they would eventually be driven out of business and the owners forced to leave. The National Socialist Women's Federation urged German women to boycott Jewish stores as a matter of principle and as proof of their patriotism. 'The German housewife in every situation of life alone can decide victory in this fight. There will not be a pfennig henceforth for a Jewish shop, for a Jewish physician or attorney from the German woman . . .' But busy women had no time to shop around for approved Aryan suppliers when their usual stores stocked all they needed.

In February 1934 Erna Günter told the readers of *NS-Frauen Warte*:

> I know that it is easier to make a quick trip to the department store. It requires thought to purchase

domestic products, remembering with each purchase that German goods provide German people with wages and food. (Erna Günter, '*Wir Frauen im Kampf um Deutschlands Erneuerung*', *NS-Frauen Warte*, 25 February 1934)

Naturally, this restriction did not apply to the wives and mistresses of the Nazi elite, who continued to do just as they pleased, buying French haute couture and Elizabeth Arden cosmetics without a second thought and flaunting their adornments at every opportunity.

Goering, Goebbels and the rest of the Hitler gang may have toadied to their Führer, but their wives were made of sterner stuff and would not be dictated to. Hitler controlled every aspect of their private and personal lives, demanding they produce a fine brood of Aryan children and that they live up to the highest moral standards, at least in public. He told them what to do and what to think, what to read and what to believe.

He could order them to leave their lovers, to refrain from smoking and wearing make-up in his presence and to marry in a Nazi-approved ceremony, forsaking their religious beliefs and renouncing their God for their Führer, but he could not influence the one thing any self-respecting woman reserves the right to determine for herself – how she dresses. Typically Hitler did not expressly forbid what he did not approve of. He merely indicated what displeased him and what qualities and mode of dress he felt embodied the ideal Aryan woman.

Unpatriotic French fashion
There was no shortage of little Hitlers, male and female, eager to implement his edicts. Agnes Gerlach, Chairwoman of the Association for German Woman's Culture, was one. She attempted to 're-educate' women through a series of articles in popular magazines, in an attempt to wean them

off inappropriate products by categorizing them as 'decadent' and 'un-German'. The 'little luxury woman' and the 'masculine woman' were unfeminine images created by the French fashion industry and its Jewish designers who were trying to corrupt the German feminine form by squeezing it into unnatural and unhealthy shapes, just as the Chinese had done to women in ancient times, binding their feet so that they would not grow beyond a certain size. Experts were drafted in to confirm such preposterous statements. Arthur Hess of the Orthopaedic Shoemakers' Trade Association provided a statement affirming that 60–70 per cent of the German population suffered from a deformity due entirely to restrictive shoes that had been designed by Jews.

Similarly, the French obsession with boyish waistlines was positively detrimental to procreation and therefore unpatriotic. The 'blurring of the sexes' was indicative of the influence of a 'foreign race'. To disfigure the big, broad-hipped German woman would be to dishonour her.

In the *National Socialist Yearbook* for 1934 Gerlach contributed an essay intended to sell the idea to Party loyalists. 'How Do I Dress Myself As A German, Tastefully and Appropriately?' informed the readers that hair dye and cosmetics were artificial aids to slow ageing. Better surely to maintain a regular exercise routine and leave nature to take its course? Constricting clothes could only lead to physical and psychological damage and ultimately to 'racial deterioration'.

> **CONSTRICTING CLOTHES COULD ONLY LEAD TO PHYSICAL AND PSYCHOLOGICAL DAMAGE AND ULTIMATELY TO 'RACIAL DETERIORATION'**

'Exhibitionism leads to deformation of the body,' she argued, as if presenting a scientific fact rather than an ideological fallacy. One had to respect cultural differences and not force one upon the other. Germany respected each of its female citizens and treated them as 'a free person', not a 'kept woman', which implied that French women only dressed to please a man and that he paid for and dictated their choice of clothes and personal appearance. In fact, it was the German leader who was dictating what women should wear, what work they should be restricted to and whose authority they must adhere to. The German woman was anything but free and the majority of them were too dazzled by their adoration of Hitler to see that they were being enslaved.

Another contributor was equally adept at twisting the truth. She snorted, 'Fashion must be individualistic – one thing is not right for everybody, especially when one nation wants to create fashion for everyone – as the French try to do it.'

One rule for the rich . . .

Magda Goebbels, for one, had no intention of playing the Teutonic warrior queen in shapeless smocks when there were French designers to dress her, Parisian milliners such as Caroline Reboux to make her stylish hats that were the envy of Marlene Dietrich, and handmade shoes by Ferragamo. She once famously declared, 'I hold it as my duty to appear as beautifully as I possibly can.' And if that meant dressing her Aryan body in clothes designed and handled by Jewish designers such as Max Becker, Richard Goetz, Paul Kuhnen and Fritz Grünfeld, then so be it. But it made her the oddest choice for President of the Reich Fashion Institute (the Deutsches Modeamt).

The Institute had been established to control, or at least attempt to influence, what German women wore and where they bought their clothes and other accessories. French fashion houses were out because Hitler hated the French; he condemned designers such as Chanel for encouraging women to cultivate the 'international silhouette' and dress in 'shapeless' unfeminine clothes with slender hips when the Aryan ideal was the fuller figure suggestive of child-bearing fertility. A slim waist was frowned upon because it was thought that thin women would be unable to bear children. In 1933 Hitler declared 'no more Paris models', which might have prompted Josef Goebbels to remove Magda from her official post at the Deutsches Modeamt.

Champagne socialist

Frau Annelies von Ribbentrop, heiress to a champagne fortune and wife of the self-important Nazi Foreign Minister, preferred English fashion. In fact, she was a committed Anglophile who insisted on furnishing her lavish home with chintz curtains and country house furniture imported from Britain. She even had English springer spaniels, which she treated more humanely than her husband. It may have been her considerable personal wealth which led her to be so condescending towards him even in company, or it may have been her nature. Whatever the reason, her behaviour earned her the epithet 'Lady Macbeth', though she was one of only three women that Hitler listened to seriously, the others being Helena Bechstein and Winifred Wagner.

Annelies had been a late convert to National Socialism, believing that Hitler was a coarse and uncultured provincial agitator. She was also suspicious of anyone who claimed to be a vegetarian and a teetotaller, but she thought it might be advantageous to play hostess to a leader who would need someone respectable like her husband to infiltrate the upper echelons of German society and, perhaps, represent them abroad. After she heard him speak her reservations evaporated. Hitler's vision for a Greater Germany stirred something inside her that gave her the feeling that everything was possible. If the Ribbentrops could prove themselves indispensable to the Party there was more than money to be made – they would be principal players in the new society. Besides, she thought it might be delicious fun to provoke her husband's notoriously liberal relations by flaunting her National Socialist credentials in public.

Annelies von Ribbentrop had been seduced by her husband's old-fashioned manners, but after providing him with five children, she realized that he did not possess the qualities she had projected on to him. He was superficial, not a man noted for his ambition and intelligence, sly rather than cunning. Nor was he popular with the 'old guard', Nazi Party members who had bloodied their hands in the days of 'the struggle'. And he was not well regarded by the leadership, though Hitler found him useful, if only because he had travelled abroad and presumably had extensive knowledge of the attitudes held by the leaders of other countries. He had also cultivated useful contacts with influential figures such as Joseph Kennedy as part of his champagne business. He was an old-fashioned charmer, not a man to initiate anything. If she wanted something, she had to organize it herself. She had tired of his constant fretting and hypochondria, those psychosomatic illnesses which he developed whenever he feared he had inadvertently offended Hitler. Even his aristocratic title had been obtained by petitioning an aunt to adopt him. As Goebbels put it, 'Von Ribbentrop bought his name, married his money and swindled his way into office.'

Hitler hoped that the Bureau would 'reflect the nature and character of the German woman' and that 'The Berlin women must become the best dressed women in Europe.' And yet he discouraged his mistress Eva Braun and the Nazi wives from wearing make-up, using hair dye, plucking their eyebrows, painting their nails or wearing furs. Whatever the Führer abhorred was frowned upon or banned. Smoking was forbidden for women in public places, where signs reminded them they risked having their cigarettes snatched out of their mouths by SA brown shirts.

Jewish tailors preferred

The Nazi hierarchy were so fearful of 'contamination' that they set up the Association of Aryan Clothing Manufacturers, which guaranteed that all materials were unsoiled by Jewish hands, a perverse marketing strategy which may have satisfied the middle and working class women who couldn't afford designer fashion (much of which was created and manufactured by Jews – it is estimated that during the 1930s, 70 per cent of the high fashion items on sale in Berlin stores were made by Jewish tailors [Source: Fabrice d'Almeida, *High Society in the Third Reich*, trans. Steven Rendall, Cambridge: Polity Press, 2008]), but high society hostesses would not be denied their luxuries. Principles be damned.

No matter how committed to the National Socialist cause they might be, the ladies of the Nazi upper class just could not bring themselves to wear the Party approved designs, no matter how much their husbands and lovers implored them to conform. They may have been suitable for the spinster aunts who ran the Nazi Women's Bureau, but no fashionable woman would have been seen dead in a Tyrolean hat and black ankle length skirt in Berlin.

Magda Goebbels and Emmy Goering continued to patronize Jewish tailor Fritz Grünfeld during the war and soon discovered that the ban on French fashion and cosmetics worked in their favour. Their high positions enabled them to ignore Nazi policy and flaunt the designer fashions and luxuries that other women were denied.

Only Gerda Bormann dressed in *Tracht* (heritage clothing) as the Reich Fashion Institute dictated. She wore her braided hair in a bun and refused to wear lipstick, in the belief that it was made from animal fat, as Hitler had stated. Every spring she was evidently pregnant with another child. She bore ten in all.

Traudl Junge described Gerda as pleasant but pale and inconspicuous, and as patient in the company of the other wives as a prisoner who knows they must endure captivity if they want to be allowed out before their sentence has been served.

Magda Goebbels

'She believed in Hitler. In her eyes he could do no wrong. It was plain to see that she swooned over him like a teenager.'
(Ariane Sheppard, Magda's half-sister)

Josef Goebbels' wife, Magda, assumed the role of 'First Lady of the Reich' with Hitler's blessing. Tall, blonde and blue-eyed, she embodied the Nazi ideal of beauty and presented herself as the matriarch of the perfect Aryan family. However, as with much in the Third Reich, appearances were deceptive.

Magda was mother to seven children, two boys and five girls, all of whom were named in honour of Hitler. Six of them were the result of her union with Goebbels (Helga, Hildegard, Helmut, Holdine, Hedwig and Heidrun), while the eldest, Harald, was the son of her first husband, wealthy industrialist Günther Quandt. For this she received the Honour Cross of the German Mother (the first recipient of this award), but she stubbornly refused to allow her eldest girls to enrol in the BdM (*Bund Deutscher Mädel*). Despite her unofficial title, she did not see the need to live according to National Socialist edicts, which determined which fashion house she should patronize and which she should boycott, nor did she agree to her children's compulsory enrolment in the Nazi Youth

> **MAGDA WAS MOTHER TO SEVEN CHILDREN, ALL OF WHOM WERE NAMED IN HONOUR OF HITLER**

organizations before they had been given a chance to experience the innocence of childhood.

Doubtful Nazi credentials

Although Magda was to achieve infamy as the mother who murdered her own children because she could not allow them to live in a world deprived of her beloved Führer, she was not an ardent Nazi.

As Wilfred von Oven, adviser to Josef Goebbels, remarked, 'She didn't actually come from a Nazi background: on the contrary, she had a strict Catholic upbringing. In no way was she a "Nazi bitch", as we used to say. Absolutely not.'

Ironically, one of the justifications Magda gave herself for committing that unspeakable act was her avowed belief in reincarnation. Magda had been introduced to Eastern philosophy by her father, engineer Oskar Ritschel, who subscribed to the Buddhist belief in the transmigration of the soul. Magda reassured herself that if her children died as 'innocents', then their spirits would not suffer but would be swiftly reborn in new bodies. She read Buddhist texts as frequently as other Nazi wives read *Mein Kampf* or the Bible, a philosophy which placed equal value on every human life as well as the lives of animals.

Stranger still, though she was married to a man who would spew forth the most virulent anti-Semitic propaganda, her beloved stepfather (her mother's second husband, Richard Friedlander) was a Jew and so too was her first love, Chaim Arlosoroff. But after her first failed marriage to wealthy German industrialist Gunther Quandt at the age of 17 (he was then 34) she found herself with nothing to live for or believe in. Then she came across the 'Nordic Circle', an exclusive club for right-wing intellectuals in Berlin, and suddenly she found a purpose. Both her mother Auguste and her second husband disapproved. Auguste remarked, 'Magda's unshakeable faith in the mission of Adolf Hitler was a complete mystery to me.'

After joining the Party in September 1930, Magda offered her talents as a translator and archivist to the Berlin headquarters and was offered a clerical post which entailed compiling a dossier of foreign news reports and recording the activities of political opponents for the city's *Gauleiter*, Josef Goebbels. She had heard him speak at the Sportpalast earlier that year and marvelled at the euphoria he whipped up despite his slight physical stature. It was the biting sarcasm and sharpness of his intellect which gave her the idea that she might like to be with this man when he scaled the heights that he was evidently destined to conquer.

Marriage to Goebbels

However, when she met Goebbels in person during her interview to discuss the creation of his personal archive, he did not make a favourable impression. 'Not a word of warmth fell from his lips,' Magda's mother recalled. 'Not a compliment. Scarcely even a personal remark.' His eyes, however, studied her intensely.

Magda was a modest but self-assured young woman who had not been above using her first husband's love letters to younger women to secure a favourable divorce settlement from him. And now she was equally determined not to become yet another plaything for the unprincipled Lothario. Goebbels' impassioned declarations of devotion were followed by expensive gifts, which unknown to Magda were paid for by her father, Oskar Ritschel. Goebbels chose them but passed the bills to Ritschel.

Goebbels was infatuated with her and professed his undying love like a romantic teenager until in July 1932 she told him about her stepfather and her first lover and most damning of all, her sympathies for the Jews and their right to a homeland of their own. Goebbels was beside himself with rage and conflicting emotions. He confessed his feelings to his diary:

> In her early life she was very irresponsible and thoughtless. And now we shall both have to pay for this. Our fate hangs on a slender thread. God grant that we are not both destroyed by her undoing . . . She's sometimes so heartless when she talks about her past. She hasn't yet completely broken with it.

Goebbels too had committed indiscretions, but had broken with a former lover, Anka Stalherm, whose mother was Jewish. Nevertheless, if it became known that the Propaganda Minister was intending to marry a woman whose stepfather was a Jew and whose first lover had been a prominent Zionist, Goebbels' career would be finished.

Whether Goebbels ordered the murder of Chaim Arlosoroff in Tel Aviv on 16 June 1933, or whether the assassins were sent by Arlosoroff's enemies in the Middle East is not known, but it is a fact that shortly after Chaim returned from a visit to Berlin to facilitate the emigration of Jews to Palestine, he was assassinated in front of his new wife by two men who were never identified or apprehended. During that final trip to Germany, Chaim had phoned Magda to ask her to use her influence with her husband and she had warned him that if he called her again it would be dangerous for both of them.

With Arlosoroff out of the way, the couple were free to marry but, as Magda had feared, her new husband could not resist a pretty face, or the chance to exercise his power over the young secretaries and film starlets whose presence he enjoyed day and night.

Infidelities
Whenever Magda learned of her husband's latest infidelity they would row until he assured her that he loved no one

else, showering her with expensive gifts and profuse apologies. As the son of a lowly bookkeeper, he needed her social standing and glamour to worm his way into high society, but as time went on she was little more than a trophy wife and he could take her loyalty for granted.

Magda was not to be sidelined. She confronted her husband with the evidence of his latest indiscretion and threatened to leave him for another man, Karl Hanke (1903–1945), an assistant in the Propaganda Ministry with whom she was having an affair out of pique more than passion. Hanke was transferred after confessing all to Goebbels, though he did not fall out of favour with Hitler who appointed him to succeed Himmler as Reichsführer-SS after 'loyal Heinrich' made peace overtures to the Allies in the last days of the war. Goebbels forgave Magda for her lack of self-control, but could not accept that he was to blame for having provoked her. Again, he brought her round not by appealing to her emotions, but by wearing down her resistance.

She told Albert Speer:

> It was frightful, the way my husband threatened me. I was just beginning to recuperate at Gastein when he turned up at the hotel. For three days he argued with me incessantly until I could no longer stand it. He used the children to blackmail me; he threatened to take them away from me. What could I do? The reconciliation is only for show . . . I'm so unhappy, but I have no choice.

She was gradually browbeaten into submission by her bully of a husband and her health deteriorated. She became prone to bouts of depression and suffered from heart problems and neuralgia, which forced her to take to her bed with splitting headaches or admit herself to a sanatorium when the attacks became unbearable. Goebbels now described her in his diary as 'hysterical', 'melodramatic', 'brainless' and 'emotional', but when in better spirits he alluded to her 'sweetness', 'loyalty' and 'courage'.

The children's nanny, Frau Hübner, witnessed the turbulent private life of the 'first family' and recalled Magda sweeping through the corridors of their Bogensee villa on the outskirts of Berlin like a prima donna, to the strains of an operatic aria echoing from the gramophone. It signalled the prelude to yet another melodramatic scene between Magda and her neurotic mother Auguste, who lived on the estate and was continually berating her daughter for marrying the 'odious' Josef. His own mother also lived in the grounds and would aggravate him by treating him like a child, her favourite phrase being 'What has that boy done now?'

Nanny Hübner remembers how Goebbels would tease his children as if he wanted to see if their affection was genuine. She thought there was something cruel about it and wondered if it might have resulted from the way he was treated by his own mother. He didn't appear to consider the feelings of his eldest daughters when he volunteered them for a morale-boosting hospital visit during the war. Helga and Hilde were traumatized after being filmed visiting severely disfigured soldiers and the footage was never used.

But Magda instilled a sense of duty in her children by having them pose for family photographs while she put on a brave front standing by her husband's side at official engagements. This was meant to reinforce the image of unity, although she was once reduced to tears at Bayreuth because of the ill treatment she suffered at the hands of her philandering husband.

Going to their deaths

It was this sense of duty which drove her to leave the comparative safety of the villa in the final weeks of the war and accompany her family to the bunker beneath the Reichschancellery, knowing that they would never leave alive.

She unburdened her feelings to her sister-in-law, Ello Quandt.

> We have demanded monstrous things from the German people, treated other nations with pitiless cruelty. For this the victors will exact their full revenge . . . we can't let them think we are cowards. Everybody else has the right to live. We haven't got this right – we have forfeited it.

Ello's insistence that a wife was not responsible for the crimes committed by her husband was dismissed out of hand.

> I make myself responsible. I belonged. I believed in Hitler and for long enough in Josef Goebbels . . . Suppose I remain alive? I should immediately be arrested and interrogated about Josef. If I tell the truth I must reveal what sort of man he was – must describe all that happened behind the scenes. Then any respectable person would turn from me in disgust . . . In the days to come Josef will be regarded as one of the greatest criminals that Germany has ever produced.

Emmy Goering

Emmy Goering vied with Magda Goebbels for the title 'First Lady of the Reich', although neither expressed their wish to be proclaimed as such. Instead they attempted to upstage each other by hosting increasingly lavish dinner parties and by dressing like royalty to outshine one another.

Ghostly rival

But Emmy Goering (born Emma Johanna Sonnemann in 1893) had a rival no wife could hope to compete with – the spectre of her husband's first wife, Carin.

Carin (b. 1888) had died of heart failure in 1931 aged 42 and had been buried in her native Sweden. But former First World War flying ace Reichsmarschall Hermann Goering, head of the Luftwaffe and deputy to Adolf Hitler, was haunted by her loss and could not live without her. So to the horror of his second wife, Emmy, he had Carin's body exhumed and transported to Germany for interment in the grounds of Carinhall, his 100,000 acre estate in the Schorfheide forest north of Berlin, named to honour her memory. In addition he built a mausoleum to house the remains and a small candlelit shrine which contained a framed photograph of his lost love, so he could talk to her when he became sentimental or morose.

Emmy, being a somewhat indulgent, pragmatic and accommodating woman, learned to live with the unseen presence and hoped that her husband would find her company more than adequate compensation.

She certainly had no reason to complain, living a life of supreme comfort in a rustic palace which boasted air-conditioned rooms and underfloor heating, though the living quarters had to be shared with Hermann's pet lion cubs, which he would exchange for younger cubs when they grew too large and aggressive. With 20 permanent staff, including cooks and 11 full-time cleaners, there was nothing for Emmy to do but enjoy herself and plan grand dinner parties. For special dinners cooks from the famous Horcher restaurant in Berlin were summoned to prepare their most celebrated dishes and guests such as the Duke and Duchess of Windsor, Charles Lindbergh and the cream of European royalty would provide lively conversation late into the night.

> **HE HAD CARIN'S BODY EXHUMED AND TRANSPORTED TO GERMANY FOR INTERMENT IN THE GROUNDS OF CARINHALL, HIS 100,000 ACRE ESTATE**

Marika Rokk was one of Germany's most popular actresses during the Nazi period. She was cast as the lead in a succession of musical films, which drew inspiration from MGM and 20th Century Fox productions. Here Rokk is pictured at the peak of her career in the 1944 musical *Die Frau meiner Träume* ('The Woman of My Dreams'). The film's sensuous costumes and risqué dance routines reportedly enraged Josef Goebbels.

With her blond hair and delicate features, Kristina Söderbaum epitomized the ideal Nazi woman. She appeared in a number of anti-Semitic films and is shown here in her most infamous role, in *Jud Süss*. In this pivotal scene Söderbaum's character, Dorothea Sturm, is forced to have sex with Jud Süß (played by Austrian actor Ferdinand Marian) in order to secure her innocent husband's release from prison.

Ilse Koch, the 'Bitch of Buchenwald', is pictured with her husband, SS Colonel Karl Koch, their son and dog. She was known for her cruelty and sadistic behaviour as an overseer in Buchenwald concentration camp – there were rumours that she collected lampshades and gloves made from the tattooed skin of dead inmates.

Herta Oberheuser, a physician at the Ravensbrück concentration camp, was the only female defendant in the Nuremberg Medical Trial. Along with 22 other doctors, Oberheuser was accused of the mass-murder of thousands of inmates. She is pictured here pleading 'not guilty' to the charges. Oberheuser was found guilty and sentenced to 20 years in jail, but was released in 1952.

Female guards photographed during the liberation of Bergen-Belsen concentration camp in April 1945:

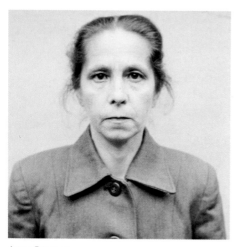

Juana Bormann
Sentenced to death, executed on 13 December, 1945

Irma Grese
Sentenced to death, executed on 13 December, 1945

Ilse Forster
Sentenced to 10 years, released
21 December, 1951

Herta Bothe
Sentenced to 10 years, released
21 December, 1951

Frieda Walter
Sentenced to 3 years, released
16 November, 1948

Anna Hempel
Sentenced to 10 years, released 21 April, 1951

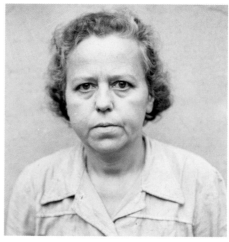

Gertrud Sauer
Sentenced to 10 years, released 21 December, 1951

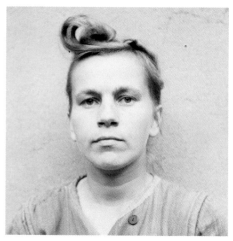

Elisabeth Volkenrath
Sentenced to death, executed on 13 December, 1945

Gertrud Feist
Sentenced to 5 years, released 11 August, 1949

Hildegard Lohbauer
Sentenced to 10 years, released
15 July, 1950

Helene Kopper
Sentenced to 15 years, released
26 February, 1952

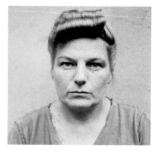

Herta Ehlert
Sentenced to 15 years, released
7 May, 1953

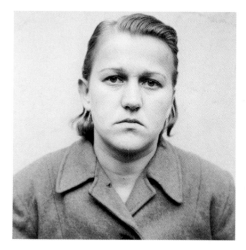

Hilde Lisiewicz
Sentenced to 1 year, released 16 November, 1946

SS women camp guards are taken to bury the dead.
The women include the Head Wardress Elisabeth
Volkenrath (partially hidden on the right) and Herta
Bothe (front left).

Known as the 'Black Angel of Ravensbrück', Carmen Mory was sentenced to death for her sadistic treatment of inmates at the women's concentration camp. She committed suicide in her cell before the sentence could be carried out.

Female prisoners are presented in the dock during the Belsen Trial in 1945. From left: (7) Elisabeth Volkenrath, (8) Herta Ehlert, (9) Irma Grese, (10) Ilse Litre and (11) Hildegard Lohbauer.

Gertraud 'Traudl' Junge, Hitler's youngest private secretary, is pictured at her wedding to Hans Junge in 1942. Junge acompanied Hitler to the Führerbunker in 1945 and typed out his will a day and a half before his suicide.

Johanna Wolf (left) was Hitler's personal secretary. She was a dedicated Nazi but, unlike Traudl Junge, refused to be interviewed after Hitler's death.

Gudrun Himmler often accompanied her father on his official duties – here she is pictured attending an indoor sports festival in March 1938.

Margarete and Gudrun Himmler, the wife and daughter of SS leader Heinrich Himmler, are pictured here in an Allied detention camp near Rome in July 1945. Gudrun (b. 1929) remains an active supporter of Neo-Nazism.

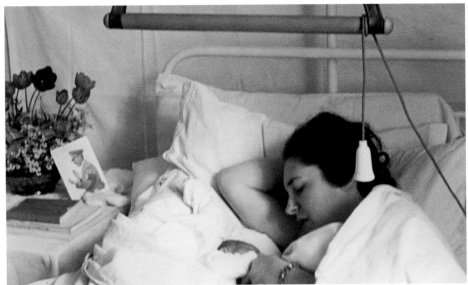

Indoctrination started young; a mother lies in her hospital bed with her new-born baby – and a portrait of Hitler at her bedside.

Emmy Goering was a stage actress before her marriage to Luftwaffe Commander-in-Chief, Hermann Goering. Here the couple are pictured leaving Berlin Cathedral on their wedding day. Hitler stands in the doorway behind them.

A little boy enjoys a Nazi lolly.

If she tired of entertaining, or listening to her husband's fireside stories about hunting, she didn't have to suffer long because he had several time-consuming obsessions with which to amuse himself. These included being fitted for new uniforms of his own design, admiring his priceless art collection stolen from the most discerning collectors, killing stags on his private estate and playing with one of two model train sets which ran the entire length of the attic and basement.

First Lady of the Reich

Emmy's efforts to be officially acknowledged as the 'First Lady of the Reich' (a title bestowed on her by Hitler himself during an informal conversation) were an attempt to live up to Hermann's image of her and only partly for her own prestige. She had been a successful stage actress at the National Theatre of Weimar, where she met her first husband, actor Karl Kostlin, in 1916, and possessed a vivacious personality that made her the perfect hostess. Emmy had no political affiliations, unlike Carin who had been a rabid anti-Semite and an early devotee of Hitler, but fate or chance contrived to bring her into Hitler's sphere of influence. The Weimar cast had frequented a popular café near the theatre and there, in 1932, Emmy met Goering, who had been widowed in the previous year.

Their first and only child was a girl, Edda, whose birth was celebrated by a flight of 500 aircraft. Her father said he would have ordered twice that number if the child had been a boy.

Hitler admired Emmy's poise and social graces, and envied the effortless ease with which she engaged guests in conversation. But she disappointed him on a number of occasions; in failing to produce more children, flouting the ban on Jewish fashion houses and, more gravely, slighting Eva Braun. Emmy's contempt for Hitler's mistress was common knowledge, but it was considered unforgivable for her to snub Braun in public. The feeling was mutual and once Goering had ceased to be the Führer's favourite it appears that Emmy became fiercely critical of Hitler and his advisers.

Falling out of favour

'Hitler was extremely charming to me until the war began,' Emmy informed an American correspondent in August 1945. Then his manner became noticeably cooler. She suspected it was because he had insisted on her marriage to Goering in 1935, because he disapproved of Nazi leaders 'leading immoral lives'. When Hitler took a mistress himself, he did not want the matter to become an embarrassment. Then after the invasion of Russia in 1941 someone told Hitler that Goering thought fighting on two fronts would lead to defeat, to which Hitler is said to have replied sternly, 'I'll take responsibility.' From that moment Goering found himself frozen out of important strategy meetings and humiliated before the generals. Hermann's visits to the front line were ridiculed by Hitler and things became so bad that Goering considered assassinating his former friend.

Himmler and Bormann were also singled out for making disparaging remarks. Both were loathed by the Goerings for toadying to Hitler, but the dictator's unbridled ego became the main topic of their private conversations. The early victories in 1939–1940 'went to his head. You can't imagine how conceited he became. My husband often said, "You can't talk to the Führer any longer."'

It was as if there was a wall between Hitler and his former comrades. He appeared to hear, but he wasn't really listening. He would agree to something then an adjutant would telephone to retract the promise because Hitler didn't have the courage to do so himself. Emmy was convinced that Hitler was mad. The continuous shaking that prevented him from keeping his right arm steady was, according to Hermann's physician Dr Ondarza, symptomatic of a 'deterioration in the brain' which also made it impossible for Hitler to pursue any thought through to its logical conclusion.

Like the wife of a man who had been passed over for promotion, Emmy sympathized with her husband's grievances. As much as Hermann revelled in the numerous titles the Führer had bestowed upon him and as much as he enjoyed strutting the world stage in ostentatious uniforms more suited to an operetta, it galled him to know that he had been succeeded in Hitler's affections by two men who hadn't earned the rank they now held. As he often reminded his wife, Himmler had escaped imprisonment after the failed putsch because he looked so unprepossessing that the police couldn't believe he was a Nazi street fighter and had let him go. Bormann, he told her, was nothing more than a jumped-up office boy, a fawning sycophant and 'boot licker' who had ingratiated himself with Hitler by arranging the funds to buy and renovate the Berghof, Hitler's private residence in the Obersalzburg.

Goering laughed bitterly every time he told her how Hans Frank, the Governor-General of Poland had said that 'hatred' was too mild a word to describe how they all felt about 'the Brown Eminence', the shadowy power behind the throne who always stood by Hitler's side in a suit at least one size too small for his bulk, perched like a vulture, waiting to interject on the Führer's behalf if anyone was taking up too much of his time.

On 6 June 1944 Hitler visited the Goering family to celebrate Edda's birthday and assured them

> **HERMANN REVELLED IN THE NUMEROUS TITLES HITLER BESTOWED ON HIM AND STRUTTED THE WORLD STAGE IN OSTENTATIOUS UNIFORMS**

both that Germany's victory was assured, despite the fact that the Allies had just landed in Normandy and had breached the first line of Fortress Europe.

She was adamant that German military leaders found Hitler 'impossible' towards the end and that the majority of the population expected her husband to succeed him. By committing suicide rather than surrendering to the Allies and answering their charges, Emmy believed that Hitler had betrayed the German people and taken the coward's way out.

Margarete Himmler

Heinrich Himmler's wife Margarete (1893–1967) was as unprepossessing as her husband. While still in her thirties she had an old woman's face and a permanent sour expression, as if she disapproved of everything. Her complexion was as colourless as her personality, leading those who had not seen her before to assume that she had recently been seriously ill and was still suffering from something which pained her greatly. She had good reason to play the long-suffering wife because her husband had embarked on a serious affair with his secretary, Hedwig Potthast, who was 12 years his junior and with whom he had two children. The affair cost him his marriage although he and Margarete did not divorce. She bore him only one child, a daughter named Güdrun whom he adored and nicknamed *Puppi* (Puppet). The devoted father took her with him on official tours including at least one visit to Dachau when she was 12. She wrote in her diary:

> Today, we went to the SS concentration camp at Dachau. We saw everything we could. We saw the gardening work. We saw the pear trees. We saw all the pictures painted by the prisoners. Marvellous. And afterwards we had a lot to eat. It was very nice.

The couple later adopted a boy but Heinrich showed little interest in him.

Himmler's attitude to women was revealed in the reports he filed in support of SS applications for marriage. Every SS officer had to submit an application for a marriage licence to the Reichsführer and abide by his decision.

Himmler denied the application of an officer identified only as 'B' on the grounds that his fiancé wore too much make-up, which made her look like a 'painted doll'. She was therefore 'entirely unsuitable', while Obersturmführer Werner K. was advised to persuade his fiancée to tone down the amount of make-up she wore and Gunner Richard A. was told that his fiancée would look more attractive if she lowered her eyebrows.

Make-up was a preoccupation of 'lesser races' and the 'foolish German women' who copy them: 'Anyone who gets herself up like a half-caste . . . is denying her own good blood.'

Himmler did not approve of the wives of SS men or their teenage daughters smoking in public. His interference in the private lives of his men knew no limits or decency. He ordered Rottenführer Z to abstain from fathering more children and advised another couple to have themselves sterilized because they were deemed to be in danger of 'hereditary impairment'.

The girls' racial origins were of particular interest to him, though the scientific basis for his conclusions was spurious at best. The shape of the skull, the colour of the eyes and the pigmentation of the skin were considered a rational basis for determining whether a potential partner would be good breeding stock for his SS supermen.

As Peter Longerich, author of the definitive biography of Himmler, notes, 'Himmler quite clearly took a strong voyeuristic interest in these procedures, as is evidenced in particular by his obsessive demand for details, and not least by his obvious curiosity with regard to female anatomy.'

But even his own men were not excluded from this irrational screening process. Obersturmführer C in the Waffen-SS was to be dismissed after the war and transferred to the Front in the interim, merely because Himmler took a dislike to the shape of the man's mouth.

His own intractable moral code and prudish insistence on correct gentlemanly behaviour was in stark and jarring contrast to his general disregard for human life and dignity, particularly in relation to the 'inferior' races and 'undesirables'. In the autumn of 1939 Gunther Tamaschke, commandant of the female concentration camp at Lichtenburg, was dismissed for neglecting his wife, though his inhuman treatment of the prisoners had merited approval.

Most bizarrely, Himmler was concerned to weed out any men who were henpecked on the grounds that 'leaders who are incapable of leading a unit of two . . . are incapable of greater things'.

Lina Heydrich

Lina Heydrich (1911–85), the unsmiling archly conservative wife of 'iron-hearted' Reinhard Heydrich, 'Hitler's Hangman', shunned haute couture as ostentatious and sinful. She thought it indicative of a vain, self-indulgent personality of which she stoutly disapproved. The daughter of a Friesian schoolteacher, she had been brought up to be modest and frugal with a preference for dressing down in sombre black and grey even when attending social functions – as if rehearsing for the role she would play for the rest of her life, that of the grieving widow who denied all knowledge of her husband's murderous work. She had no ambitions of her own other than to promote National Socialism, in which she fervently believed. In fact, it was her ruthless desire to see the Party implement the removal of the Jews from society that 'radicalized' her husband and prompted him to join the SS.

'We felt provoked by the Jews,' she wrote in the 1970s, 'and we simply felt that we had to hate them.' During the first weeks of their courtship she was horrified to hear that Heydrich had not read *Mein Kampf* and that he regarded the Nazi leaders as a joke. He called them 'privates from Bohemia' and wanted nothing to do with them, but his own mother sided with Lina in urging him to join, in the belief that securing an influential position would be the making of him. In the end, it was Lina's persistence that persuaded him to pursue a career with the Nazis.

It was she who urged him to apply to join the SS after his dishonourable dismissal from the navy and it was her idea that he should falsely present himself as a former navy intelligence officer, when in fact he had been a mere cadet. When Himmler cancelled their first meeting on a pretext, Lina packed her husband's bag and saw him aboard the train to Munich. At that crucial interview on 14 June 1931, Himmler tested the applicant's suitability by asking him to draw up a plan for a counter-intelligence division. Heydrich pulled together everything he had picked up during his brief time in the navy and padded it out with suitably sinister-sounding notions he had read in cheap detective novels and spy stories as a boy. It seemed to satisfy Himmler who offered Heydrich the post there and then.

Thereafter Lina derived grim satisfaction from Heydrich's advancement in the organization although he earned only 180 marks a month, considerably lower than a construction worker.

As Chief of the Reich Main Security Office (RSHA), Heydrich chaired the Wannsee Conference in Berlin in January 1942, at which the fate of millions of Jews was decided within a few hours. After that he was charged by

Hitler with overseeing the liquidation of the ghettos in occupied Poland, which earned him his final posting as Deputy Protector of Bohemia and Moravia in the former Czechoslovakia. Within weeks of his arrival he ordered the murder of 400 civilians to establish his authority or, as he put it, because he needed his 'quiet space'.

Not so merry widow

Lina was fiercely proud of her husband and it could be said that she lived her life vicariously through him. It is telling that she described the initial interview with Himmler as 'the finest hour of my life'. But she resented his prolonged absences, which put a serious strain on their marriage. She may have appeared austere but she was not above flirting with one of her husband's commanding officers, Walter Schellenberg, in order to force her husband to pay more attention to her. After the rumours of her affair reached Heydrich he returned and they cemented their commitment with the fourth of four children, Marte, who was born shortly after Heydrich's assassination in 1942. It is rumoured that Himmler became more attentive to her after the death of her husband than she would have liked and that he had a struggle to keep her from assuming a more prominent role as the wife of a Nazi 'martyr'.

IF HEYDRICH HAD THE ARROGANCE TO RIDE THROUGH PRAGUE IN AN OPEN-TOPPED, UNARMOURED CAR HE ONLY HAD HIS OWN 'STUPIDITY' TO BLAME

Her demand for an increase in her widow's pension became an issue. She insisted that she should receive an extra payment because Heydrich had been killed in the defence of his country, while Hitler – who had made a show of his sorrow at the state funeral of his 'loyal Protector' – dismissed her appeal out of hand. If Heydrich had the arrogance to ride through the streets of occupied Prague in an open-topped, unarmoured car, Hitler told his inner circle, then he only had his own 'stupidity' to blame for the result. Lina then wrangled with the Reichsführer-SS over payments due for work done on her property, which had been carried out by concentration camp inmates.

Keeping the peace

Himmler's former chief of staff, Karl Wolff, was given the unenviable task of isolating Lina from Nazi society by offering her a rehabilitative holiday at the palatial Park Hotel in Merano, Italy in the summer of 1944. As if fighting a losing war was not enough, Wolff was assigned the onerous task of keeping Lina and her mother-in-law from making a scene at the resort. 'Mother Heydrich is a good woman,' Himmler told Wolff, 'however, she has never in her life been able to keep herself busy.' Wolff was warned that he would have to keep the peace not only between Lina and 'Mother Heydrich' but also between Lina and the old woman's son-in-law Heindorf and his wife, Heydrich's sister. Lina was eventually compensated with an estate in Bohemia that had been 'confiscated' from its Jewish owner. However, Himmler delayed authorizing the transfer and consequently when the Russians arrived Lina and her children found themselves homeless, but not for long.

After the war she married a Finnish theatre director in order to change her surname, because of the negative attention it attracted, and she published her autobiography *Life With A War Criminal* (1976) which, despite the title, made no apology for Heydrich's crimes.

Margarete Speer

In contrast, Hitler's architect and Armaments Minister Albert Speer made a second and very lucrative career as an apologist, a professional penitent whose seeming willingness to 'come clean' in public (preferably on TV chat shows to promote his two best-selling books) made him the acceptable face of Nazism and a very marketable one at that. Speer was aided in his denial by his wife, Margarete, a slender, petite, blue-eyed blonde with whom he had an unspoken understanding regarding the 'difficult' subjects that were never to be raised behind the walls of their immaculate Heidelberg villa. She found it expedient to present a look of trusting innocence to avoid having to comment on 'political' matters of which she couldn't be expected to have any personal knowledge. In that respect she was the perfect Nazi wife: loyal, reserved, unquestioningly obedient and physically inconspicuous. Her reluctance to display any strong interest or emotion above childlike curiosity made it easier for her husband to protest his innocence and absolve himself of all responsibility for the ill-treatment of the slave labourers who were starved, beaten and worked to death in the factories and military facilities over which he presided.

She made him the perfect mate, her ingenuousness meshing with his emotional frigidity. He knew that what the regime was doing was barbaric and inhumane, but he simply could not feel compassion for those who suffered.

Dr Carol Rittner, Distinguished Professor of Holocaust and Genocide Studies at the Richard Stockton College of New Jersey, contends that women such as Margarete Speer, 'cultivated their own private worlds of pleasure. They gossiped, enjoyed arts and films, took care of their homes and children, entertained, socialized, looked after their husbands and carefully avoided asking difficult questions.'

Taboo subject

The artificial conviviality of the Berghof was disturbed only once, when Henriette von Schirach broached a topic that was strictly taboo. One evening in 1943, as the guests waited for someone to speak, Henny asked if her host was aware of what was happening to the Jews. 'Mein Führer, I saw a train full of deported Jews in Amsterdam the other day. Those poor people – they look terrible. I'm sure they're being very badly treated. Do you know about it? Do you allow it?' After a silence, Hitler answered:

> Be silent, Frau von Schirach, you understand nothing about it. You are sentimental. What does it matter to you what happens to female Jews? Every day tens of thousands of my most valuable men fall while the inferior survive. In that way the balance in Europe is being undermined [. . .] And what will become of Europe in one hundred, in one thousand, years?

When Hitler became morose, her husband interjected with a few observations of his own in the hope of breaking the awkward silence. He told the American psychologist Dr Gilbert after the war what happened next. 'He flew at me with such rage that I thought I would surely be arrested. I fell from grace after that.'

Art collector

No one raised the subject again in the Führer's presence and all professed to be ignorant of events that were unfolding outside their insulated circle, but Emmy Goering was certainly aware of the crimes her husband was engaging in. Hermann had amassed a museum's worth of priceless art treasures, which were on display at their home, Carinhall, north of Berlin, and it was an open secret that he had 'confiscated' them from Jewish art dealers and wealthy families in return for an exit visa and safe passage to a neutral country. In some cases he had the effrontery to offer them a receipt for the 'loan' of paintings and statues, while in others he had asked for an invoice that he never intended to pay. But the loot was not the only evidence Emmy was aware of. She was privy to conversations between Hermann and his stepbrother Albert, who was frequently arrested by the Gestapo for intervening on behalf of persecuted Jews. And her husband would have complained long and bitterly about the trouble Albert was giving him by provoking the authorities in this way.

Final Solution supporter

But as a rule, the wives didn't ask awkward questions or even show any interest in their husband's activities. Gerda Bormann, wife of Martin Bormann, Hitler's personal secretary, was however, an exception. Her private correspondence reveals a detailed knowledge of the genocide and her support for the implementation of the Final Solution. But then, Gerda was the only top Nazi wife who embraced the ideology with real enthusiasm. In September 1944, she wrote:

> It cannot possibly be the meaning of history that Jewry should make itself the master of the world. It is terrible how powerful it is everywhere. And whatever way the war ends, it will always mean a strengthening of the Jewish stock and the Jewish purse. The Jews don't spill their blood in battle, they manage to get away from the danger of bombs . . . and even during revolts and guerrilla fighting they only egg the others on from safe hide-outs. Disease and dirt cannot hurt that vermin. So, how shall they ever get reduced in numbers?

It is clear that she had swallowed the lie that the ills of the world were created by an all-powerful, invisible cabal.

> As Goebbels says – we aren't fighting the three Great Powers, but a single power that is behind them, something that is much worse, and this is the reason why

I can't at present imagine how we shall get peace ever, even if we win the war.

Knowing that his wife took an active interest in the progress of the eradication of the Jews and in policy matters in general, her husband would occasionally include copies of private memos and other documents to keep Gerda up to date. He would also keep her informed of the various personalities and officials whom he had met and his impression of them. He would emphasize how hard he was working, giving her details of the meetings he had attended and what long hours he had been forced to put in. This was offered partly to prove how indispensable he had become after replacing Rudolf Hess as Hitler's private secretary and partly to keep her informed of developments that he knew she was concerned about.

The 'Queen Mother'

Luise Funk, wife of Economic Minister Walther Funk, was a frumpy, nervous, self-conscious type, always chattering to hide her anxiety, and adorning herself like a cheap Christmas ornament – with rouged cheeks and dyed red hair and her fingers weighed down with tacky rings.

In contrast, Baroness Marie Auguste von Neurath (1875–1960), the wife of Konstantin von Neurath, Hitler's first Foreign Minister, was renowned for her imperious, condescending manner and her fondness for wearing pearls and a tiara to every official function, which earned her the title 'the Queen Mother'. But she was a genuine aristocrat and no one had the nerve to tell her that wearing a fox fur stole to a reception was overdoing it.

Neurath was a diplomat of the old school and inclined to believe that every Reichstag member was a gentleman whose word could be trusted, but he naïvely believed that the SA would be brought to heel once the Party was in power. Had he protested at the Nazis' deplorable tactics

VON NEURATH DEFENDED THE EXTERMINATION OF THE JEWS BY SAYING THAT THEY HAD ENJOYED TOO MUCH INFLUENCE IN GERMANY

during the first 18 months of Hitler's chancellorship and threatened to resign, he might have encouraged President von Hindenburg to demand Hitler's expulsion from office.

He and his wife were treated by the Nazi hierarchy as gullible old duffers who would prove useful in presenting a respectable façade for the new administration. They could be relied upon to support its seizure of territory in the interwar years and its anti-Semitic laws in the face of foreign condemnation. On 2 April 1933 Neurath thanked Mussolini's fascist Italian government for defending Germany's boycott of Jewish businesses and damning negative foreign press reports as sensationalist propaganda. At Nuremberg he defended the extermination of the Jews by saying that they had enjoyed too much influence in Germany and that it was necessary to purge them from public life. The Baron's wilful disregard for reality was encapsulated in his answer to British prosecutor Sir David Maxwell-Fyfe, who asked the old man why he continued to support a government that used murder as a means of political action. Neurath's response was 'such mishaps cannot be avoided'.

CHAPTER SEVEN

Resisting Evil

Not all German women gave in to Nazi tyranny. Some resisted by aiding the Jews, others avoided giving the Hitler salute or demonstrated in public . . .

She looked like any other young mother pushing her pram through the streets of Brandenburg with her eldest child, a lively four-year-old, skipping alongside. The men acknowledged her with a polite nod and a customary 'Guten Tag' or 'Guten Morgen, Frau Vetter', and the women beamed approvingly at the petite auburn-haired 30-year-old and her well brought up daughter, who gave the Hitler salute to every neighbour they passed. There goes a model Aryan mother they told each other. The Führer would be proud.

Escaping the round-up

But Frau Vetter was not an Aryan. According to the Nazi race laws she was not even a German, but a Jew, and she was living in the lion's den under a false name. Living and working in open defiance of the Nuremberg Laws and other Nazi racial decrees which demanded that she wore a yellow star, walked in the gutter and lowered her eyes in deference to every SA and SS man she encountered on the street.

Goebbels had boasted that Germany was *judenfrei*, but it was another lie. Grete Vetter should have been transported to Auschwitz with her widowed mother, assuming the old woman had left the ghetto alive. Instead she was now what was commonly known as a 'U-boat', an enemy of the state living underground, undetected and in constant fear of being betrayed. So afraid, in fact, that she had refused to accept pain killers during the birth of her baby in case the drug had loosened her tongue and she had given herself away in her delirium. Grete had heard other women blurt out their most intimate secrets under the influence of the anaesthetic when she had worked as a Red Cross nurse, the only organization she could risk working for because their volunteers were exempt from security checks. She had heard one patient cry out the name of her illicit lover and the true father of her child, a Polish slave worker. Interracial relations – *Rassenschande* – were strictly forbidden and discovery would have meant death for the father, mother and baby. Another confessed to hearing her soldier son's voice on Radio Moscow after he had been captured by the Russians, when listening to foreign stations was punishable by imprisonment. Better to suffer the pain, Grete had told herself, than risk betraying the friends who had risked their lives to help you.

> **SHE WAS NOW WHAT WAS COMMONLY KNOWN AS A 'U-BOAT', AN ENEMY OF THE STATE LIVING UNDERGROUND**

No, the Führer would not have been proud, he would have been apoplectic had he known such people had evaded his brutal, systematic round-ups. More so if he had seen that Grete and her anonymous, invisible companions defied the way Nazi propaganda had depicted them, as vermin scurrying through the sewers in *The Eternal Jew*, or as vile caricatures in the pages of *Der Stürmer*, grasping greedily at virtuous Aryan girls. Grete, her family and friends were disgusted by such crude assaults on their character and despaired when they saw how readily their once friendly neighbours had joined in the Jew baiting, the boycotting of Jewish businesses and the segregation of cafés, restaurants and other public places. She was well-educated, conscientious, cultured and had been only weeks away from qualifying as a lawyer before the university barred her from taking the final exam, forcing her to work as a Red Cross nurse under an assumed name to avoid the round-up.

The little girl trotting happily beside her was not her daughter but her stepdaughter, who was staying with Grete and her fiancé so that he could qualify for visiting rights. Her real mother had taught her to 'Heil Hitler' everyone in sight, a mother who had no idea that her darling Barbl was in the care of a fugitive Jewess. She had no reason to suspect she had been deceived. Even the grey-faced state official who issued marriage licences in Brandenburg had been fooled into providing the life-saving *deutschblütig* (German Blood) rubber stamp of approval without the required documentation. He told her: 'Well, it is obvious just from looking at you that you could not possibly be anything but a pure-blooded Aryan.'

Marriage to a German soldier

Grete had managed to pass herself off as an Aryan by virtue of what she called her 'typical Austrian features', a set of borrowed identity papers and the most extraordinary stroke of good fortune a Jewess in Nazi Germany could have hoped for – provided she could bring herself to live a lie and keep her nerve. She had been courted by a German soldier who genuinely loved her and had offered to marry her, even after she had entrusted him with her dreadful secret.

She was not a collaborator and an opportunist like the girls in the occupied territories, who became the mistresses of German soldiers in order to share the luxuries and privileges that their fellow countrymen were denied. No, she was truly infatuated with the man behind the uniform. She told herself that he was a mere supervisor in the paint department of an aircraft factory and had never fired a shot in anger. (He was exempt from military service due to blindness in one eye but he would later be promoted and sent to the Eastern Front, where he was captured and imprisoned by the Soviets.)

Thirty-five per cent of the workers at the plant were from the conquered countries ('a group not especially motivated to break production records for the Luftwaffe') and only because the Nazis could not spare German women to work in the factories. 'The pram is the tank of the home front,' barked one ministry slogan and by the summer of 1944 it was too late to reverse their policy and make up the shortfall in armaments production. Hitler's fantasy of heroes and Hausfraus would contribute to their rapid defeat. The remainder of Werner's colleagues were old men, young boys and girls who chose to get themselves pregnant to avoid the monotonous routine and not, as Hitler had hoped, to raise blond, blue-eyed Aryan babies to fight for the Fatherland.

After she moved in with him, Grete and Werner enjoyed a normal life, albeit one sustained on wartime rations. The allowance for married couples was: 150 grams of meat, 50 grams of butter, 40 grams of oil, 200 grams of bread, 50 grams of cereal, 100 grams of sugar, 25 grams of coffee substitute, one egg per wedding guest and a copy of *Mein Kampf* – only in the week they made their union official the local Party office had run out of copies.

Tuning in to the truth

They listened in the dark to the BBC and heard the true cost of Germany's hubris – the defeat at Stalingrad and the Allies' steady advance through France. Then one day Grete recognized a familiar call note coming from a neighbour's apartment and realized that they too were listening to the forbidden broadcasts. While Germany gobbled up its neighbours they all wanted to share the spoils, but as soon as the tide turned, many realized there would be a terrible price to pay. Even Goebbels, that master of manipulation and misdirection, could not fool all of the people all of the time.

Starved of real news, loyal German citizens were turning the dial to hear the facts. In public they gave the Hitler salute. In private many were asking themselves if they were being told the truth or just what the regime wanted them to hear. Werner made himself popular at the factory by repeating the latest Party lie – 'Churchill was an alcoholic and an aristocrat who was not loved by the people like the Führer' and 'the Führer knows best' – but at home he lived with a Jewish fugitive and listened to the BBC because he knew he could not trust the official German station. 'To live in ignorance,' she decided, 'all you had to do was listen only to the Nazi news.'

Grete and Werner were like any other two people in love. Only they had the misfortune to have been born at a time and in a place where all reason appeared to have been suspended – at least for the time being. 'To this day,' Grete (whose real name was Edith Hahn) wrote, 'I cannot understand what made Werner Vetter so brave when his countrymen were so craven.' She came to the conclusion that he had a problem with authority and that lying to his superiors was his way of breaking free. The fact that he lived in the most authoritarian regime in history gave him leave to tell bigger lies. He would tell his bosses that he had to take a day off because his mother's house had been bombed and when he felt like another day off work he would inform them that her new house had been hit. It gratified him to think that he was enjoying himself while they were working. No one questioned him. He had a talent for it. And she suspected that his interest in her was partly the thrill of living the most outrageous lie of all.

Adapting to life under tyranny

Living as a German Hausfrau in the heart of the Reich gave Grete a unique opportunity to observe how her female colleagues and neighbours adapted to life under tyranny.

Paying lip service

An acquaintance who had joined the Party early on had been rewarded for her loyalty with a shop that had once belonged to a Jewish proprietor. But she had assisted Jewish families to leave Germany because her life had once been saved by a Jewish doctor and she felt obliged to repay the debt. Grete considered her a 'fine woman' and was astonished to learn that she had joined the Party not out of conviction but simply to marry the man she loved, who was prevented by the Catholic Church from divorcing his wife. The Nazis had promised to repeal the divorce laws and so Frau Niederall had signed up and paid her dues. And when Grete had torn the yellow star from her coat the only person she felt she could turn to was Frau Niederall, who sent her to a sympathetic *Sippenforscher*, a Racial Affairs official, who gave Grete specific instructions on what documents she would need and how she could obtain them. How many other sound German citizens, she wondered, only paid lip service to the Party?

Another woman had compromised her convictions for an even more trivial reason. Hilde Schlegel, a neighbour, had joined the Party after she had been taken to a Nazi banquet where they served buttered rolls. It was the first time she had tasted butter and, for a 15-year-old girl who had known nothing but poverty, hunger and charity hand-outs, it was enough to persuade her that National Socialism had the best interests of the people at heart. 'I think everything we have we owe our dear Führer,' she told Grete, as they toasted his health over tea.

No one knows how many practised the Zen-like attitude of detachment and passive resistance known as 'internal emigration' (a term coined by German writer Erich Kästner), but as much as they might have liked to believe that it was a form of passive resistance, it didn't prevent one bomb from being dropped by the Luftwaffe or one bullet from being fired by a German soldier.

She noted the mood of defeatism that fell like a pall over Germany after the debacle at Stalingrad, when families were urged by Goebbels to live on a single one-plate evening meal. She also witnessed the small acts of defiance they would engage in and overheard them blithely repeat the preposterous lies they had accepted as fact.

Uncaring profession

Her nursing colleagues believed that the shortage of onions was due to them being used to make poison gas. By May 1943 they had become a luxury. When Grete caught one of the senior nurses feeding an onion to a dying Russian prisoner in defiance of strict orders to give them only basic rations, the woman appeared afraid that Grete would denounce her to the Gestapo. She had bought the onion on the black market for her patient's last meal, knowing that to do so risked imprisonment. But she was an exception. More typically, the staff stole the food meant for the foreign patients, having been indoctrinated by Nazi propaganda to believe that it was their right to do so. When an entire building had been set aside for typhus patients, the nurses assumed the foreign slave workers had become infected because of their 'filthy personal habits' and not because they had been kept in unhygienic conditions and infected

> **THE STAFF STOLE THE FOOD MEANT FOR THE FOREIGN PATIENTS, HAVING BEEN INDOCTRINATED TO BELIEVE THAT IT WAS THEIR RIGHT TO DO SO**

by contaminated water supplied by their 'superior' German masters.

For many of the young girls who had volunteered to staff the wards at the *Städtische Krankenhaus* (City Hospital), nursing was not seen as a caring profession, but as a means of escaping a hard life working on their parents' farms in East Prussia. They were unskilled, little better than cleaning women, as one surgeon put it, fit only for emptying bedpans, changing dressings and administering medicine. In the morning, they were taught the rudiments of first aid by professional nurses and in the afternoon they attended compulsory classes in Nazi doctrine organized by the *NS-Frauenschaft*, the auxiliary women's arm of the Nazi Party.

This was the young nurses' real mission – to boost their patients' morale so that every wounded German soldier would want to return to the Front, convinced of his invincibility. Blatantly false reports were fed to Grete and her colleagues for them to pass on as fact and every inducement was offered to tempt the girls to Germanize occupied areas of Poland. They were promised an estate of their own to manage and a free local labour force who 'understood' that their purpose was to work for their German masters. Thousands migrated to Vartegau to raise families and populate Poland with Nazi clones, only to return as destitute refugees when the war was lost, begging in vain for sympathy and a hot meal.

Keeping a low profile

In the German Red Cross compassion was not encouraged. As a punishment for being too kind to her patients and conversing in their own language, Grete was transferred to a maternity unit and there too she had to constrain her natural intelligence, affect a harmless demeanour and make herself as inconspicuous as possible. She dressed neatly but wore little or no make-up so as not to attract attention. And when the prickly subject of Party membership was raised, she pretended to be so slow and simple-minded that it was her memory and not her convictions that were questioned. Surviving on her wits, but never revealing that she possessed more than might be expected from a young woman in her profession, she fended off potentially dangerous probing questions with a disarming answer that seemed to satisfy her interrogators and allow her to live another day.

When Berlin's wives protested

Anti-Nazi protests were unheard of during the Third Reich – at least that is the impression given in the conventional histories of the period. But protests did take place and, most remarkably, in the very heart of the dictatorship – on the streets of Berlin.

On 18 February 1943, after the Sixth Army's surrender at Stalingrad, Goebbels declared 'total war' against the Allies in a speech at the Sportpalast. The Jews of Berlin, who up to now had been spared transportation to the extermination camps because the regime feared that the round-up might reach the ears of international news agencies based in the capital, were arrested on 27 February by a contingent of SS and Gestapo members and taken to the Jewish Administration Building in Rosenstrasse. Among them were the Jewish spouses of non-Jewish German nationals, who had been allowed to remain in the city due to the essential nature of their work and for whom special dispensation had been granted to ensure their co-operation. The children of these intermarriages were also taken.

But news of the arrests spread swiftly and soon more than a hundred women were gathered in the street demanding the release of their husbands and children. When they were refused entry, they asked to be given proof that their loved ones were inside and they informed the guards that they would remain outside until all were released. The brother-in-law of one of the men who had been arrested told the SS that he was on leave from the army and would not be returning to the Front until his sister's husband had been released. But even this was not sufficient to persuade those in charge to free their prisoners.

If the SS and the Gestapo thought the crowd would melt away when darkness came, they were soon disappointed. To keep their spirits up the protesters linked arms and began chanting, 'Let our husbands go!', which aroused the interest of the London correspondents, who sent a report to the BBC citing the demonstration as proof that the fascist state was not as indomitable as it had portrayed itself and that the first signs of dissent were evident for all to see.

By late on the second morning the crowd of women had grown to more than 600 and they were increasingly vocal, which left the Gestapo and their SS escorts at a loss as to what to do. German civilians had never publicly defied them before and certainly not in such numbers. There were too many to be arrested and they couldn't be fired upon as all the women were German citizens. They were determined to stand their ground and wouldn't be threatened.

It may have been a spontaneous demonstration, but these particular women had never been passive supporters of the Nazi state. Many had written letters to various departments in the past objecting to measures they hadn't agreed with, specifically the theft of Jewish property by the state, the laws which forbade Jews from the professions and from intermarrying.

But clearly the stand-off couldn't continue with the foreign press looking on. On the third day the SS fired several volleys wide of the women, sending them running for cover. But they always returned, certain that the soldiers wouldn't shoot German women. It would not be easy for the SS to intimidate them or persuade them to disperse.

In the following days the protesters were joined by fellow Berliners who were sympathetic to their cause, including some of the city's intellectuals who had always considered the Nazis coarse, rabble-rousing extremists. Before the week was out the crowd had swelled to more than a thousand and a few felt brave enough to shout abuse at the SS. Attempts by the authorities to prevent more from joining the protest by restricting public transport to Rosenstrasse failed, as supporters simply walked the extra distance. It had all the makings of a very public humiliation for the regime who, on 6 March, were finally forced to release some 1,700 prisoners, including 35 men that had already been transported to Auschwitz.

The following day a witness, Ruth Andreas Friedrich, wrote in her diary:

> Six thousand non-Jewish women pushed into the Rosenstrasse [. . .] Six thousand women called for their men, screamed for their men, wailed for their men. Stood like a wall. Hour after hour. Night and day [. . .] At noon on Monday comes the decision from the headquarters of the SS [. . .] Those lucky enough to have married a non-Jewish partner may pack their bags and go home.

Had the women of Germany done the same for their fellow citizens in the first years of the dictatorship, millions might have been saved from extermination.

In the following days it is believed that Goebbels made it known that Jews in Berlin were required to take off the mandatory yellow star so that he could tell Hitler that the capital was *judenfrei* (free of Jews).

The Rosenstrasse protest was not the only demonstration against the state organized by German women. On

11 October that year the inhabitants of Witten were ordered to evacuate their homes by officials who feared they would be killed by Allied air raids. When many refused their food ration cards were withheld, which prompted approximately 300 women of the town to go into the main square to protest. These very public demonstrations quickly spread to Bochum, Hamm and Lünen, meaning the regional authorities had to refrain from 'coercive measures' to control the population.

Lilly Wust

Other otherwise unexceptional women made their own quiet but significant protest, not out of political conviction but simply because they knew that they couldn't have lived with themselves if they hadn't acted to help a fellow human being when the opportunity presented itself.

Charlotte Elisabeth Wust was the 30-year-old wife of a German army officer and the mother of four sons, which earned her the coveted bronze medal from the state. But in 1942, while her husband was at the Front, 'Lilly' met and fell in love with another woman, Felice Schragenheim, an editorial assistant with a pro-Nazi publisher, and the two women became intimate.

'It was the tenderest love you could imagine,' she later recalled. 'I was fairly experienced with men, but with Felice I reached a far deeper understanding of sex than ever before. There was an immediate attraction, and we flirted outrageously. I began to feel alive as I never had before.'

Felice was her 'better half', her 'reflection' and it seemed only natural that they should marry later that summer in a private ceremony that they formulated to make their commitment binding. Theirs was a secret love that would have had serious consequences had it been reported to the Gestapo for, unknown to Lilly, her lover was not only a Jew but an active member of the underground resistance. It was only after the jealous Lilly quizzed her about a prolonged absence that Felice confessed to organizing safe houses for German Jews who needed an escape route to neutral Switzerland. Lilly remembered, 'She told me she was a Jew and immediately I took her in my arms, and I loved her even more.'

FELICE CONFESSED TO ORGANIZING SAFE HOUSES FOR GERMAN JEWS WHO NEEDED AN ESCAPE ROUTE TO NEUTRAL SWITZERLAND

The next few months were fraught with danger and the fear that a neighbour might denounce them. Every knock on the front door, every approaching vehicle had their hearts racing. They remained inside the apartment playing with the children, talking about their shared love of literature and charting the course of the German retreat on a large wall map.

Although Lilly had begun married life as an admirer of Hitler, she had come to question and then to loathe the Nazis and all that they stood for. She and Felice knew the risks they were running but it was only when Felice was arrested and deported to Theresienstadt concentration camp that Lilly found the courage she never suspected she possessed. She took an extraordinary risk to visit her friend and see if she could persuade the commandant to release her. But an SS officer became suspicious and told her that if it hadn't been for the fact that her children needed a mother, he would have had her imprisoned too. On her return home Lilly made a silent vow to continue her lover's work by offering sanctuary to other Jewish women in the lesbian community.

The couple corresponded for over a year, with Felice signing herself 'Your caged Jaguar' in letters smuggled out of the camp until Boxing Day 1944, after which Lilly's letters were never returned. For four years Lilly tried to discover what had become of her lover. When she finally learned that Felice had died of tuberculosis five days after that final note she gave in to depression and attempted suicide, only to be saved by a friend.

She divorced her husband and thereafter lived alone, allowing herself one day a week – every Sunday – to remember Felice, whom she had never stopped loving.

In September 1981 she was awarded the Order of the Federal Republic of Germany for offering shelter to the Jewish women, all of whom had survived the war. But once her secret was out she suffered abuse and harassment from neo-Nazis. Ironically, it was their threats which prompted her to tell her story to an Austrian journalist, Erica Fisher, which was subsequently published and then dramatized in the film *Aimée & Jaguar* (1999), the pet names they had given each other at the start of their relationship. Lilly told a reporter:

> I suddenly felt that I owed it to Felice, so that people would know who she was. Twice since she left, I've felt her breath, and a warm presence next to me. I dream that we will meet again – I live in hope.

Despite the periodic intimidation she remained in Berlin until her death in 2006, aged 92. In 1995 Lilly was acknowledged as one of the Righteous Among the Nations by Yad Vashem, the World Center for Holocaust Research, an honour previously bestowed on Oskar Schindler and Raoul Wallenberg.

Berlin's dissenters

Berlin was a cosmopolitan community, many of whose inhabitants considered themselves a breed apart from their fellow countrymen. The capital's voters had firmly rejected the Nazis in the last election before Hitler seized power and its young women had no intention of leaving the night clubs and cabarets to submit to a life of domestic slavery to placate their new masters. Over 1,500 were honoured as 'Unsung Heroes' by the Senator for the Interior for West Berlin between 1958 and 1963, in recognition of their selfless action in saving lives. The majority of these were women.

Often female resistance was expressed in small acts of defiance, a favourite one being the carrying of two shopping bags when one would have been enough, to give the woman an excuse for not having an arm free to give local officials the Nazi salute.

Maria's charity

In the winter of 1942, Berlin housewife Maria Nickel, a 32-year-old mother of two, observed a heavily pregnant young woman walking to work, a yellow star stitched to her threadbare jacket.

For several days Maria followed the girl, uncertain how to approach her, unsure about what she could do for her. But something nagged at her, urging her to intervene regardless of the risk in helping a Jew, an offence punishable by imprisonment and the loss of her children.

On the third or fourth day, Maria plucked up the courage and blurted out that she wanted to help, only to have the girl run away calling to be left alone. But Maria would not be put off. One day she appeared at the factory where the girl, Ruth Abraham, was forced to work with other Jews under Nazi guard and offered her a basket of food with the words, 'Take this, I cannot enjoy Christmas with my family, knowing that you are carrying this baby and don't have enough to eat.'

Maria's charity was not an act of spontaneity, but had been fermenting for some time. Ever since she had seen German officers refuse food to starving Jewish children, Maria had sworn that she would help the next Jewish person she saw. Ruth soon learned that Maria's

offer was genuine and she could be trusted and so when the baby, Reha, was born in January 1943, Ruth reluctantly agreed to let Maria raise it as her own until she was able to look after it. But it wasn't simply a question of safety. As the infant's legal mother, Maria was able to obtain medication and attend a regular clinic. She also obtained Aryan papers for Ruth and her husband Walter by applying for a postal ID in her own name with a photo of Ruth in place of her own and giving Walter her husband's driving licence. Unfortunately, the new papers were seized and Maria and her husband Willy were summoned to Gestapo headquarters in Prinz Albrecht Strasse, a building from which many Berlin citizens never left alive. At this point Maria confided in her husband and told him their only hope was to plead ignorance. Unable to find a link between the Abrahams and the Nickels, the Gestapo let Maria and Willy off with a warning that any contact with Jews would mean they would lose their children and face imprisonment for committing *Judenhilfe* (assisting Jews).

The Nickels were not intimidated and continued to protect Reha until she was reunited with her natural parents after the war. In 1971 Maria was recognized by Yad Vashem as One of the Righteous Among the Nations.

A British Berliner's anguish

Christabel Bielenberg, the British-born wife of a German lawyer who was living in Berlin in early 1943, was another female victim of Hitler's regime, and although her suffering was psychological rather than physical, the memory of her inability to save a Jewish couple from certain death haunted her to the end of her days. She sheltered them for two days at great risk to herself and her own family, but could not risk a third. 'I simply could not say "no",' she recalled. On the morning of the third day Christabel discovered that they had cleaned the cellar so that no trace of their stay would give her away. She later learned that they had been caught at a nearby railway station and transported to Auschwitz.

'I realized then that Hitler had turned me into a murderer.'

Speaking out against despotism

Occasionally a courageous person would speak out spontaneously with no thought for the consequences, though to do so would be to risk imprisonment or worse. Berlin Hausfrau Emmi Bonhoeffer remembered that her brother-in-law had made a disparaging remark on seeing a burning synagogue the morning after *Kristallnacht*, to the effect that such destruction brought shame to the German people. He was overheard by a plain clothes Gestapo agent, who ordered her brother-in-law to appear at Gestapo headquarters the next morning. His punishment was to distribute ration cards in the neighbourhood once a month for the next seven years, until the end of the war.

> **OCCASIONALLY A COURAGEOUS PERSON WOULD SPEAK OUT SPONTANEOUSLY WITH NO THOUGHT FOR THE CONSEQUENCES**

'The family had to arrange the cards for each category of the population,' Emmi remembered, 'workers, children, etc., but he was not permitted to have a helper. He had to go alone. That was how they broke the back of the people.'

Emmi later told her neighbours what she had heard was happening in the concentration camps, but they refused to believe her 'horror stories'. It was Allied propaganda, they said. When she told her husband Klaus what she had done he warned her that she was putting their family in the gravest danger. He told her that a dictatorship is like a snake – if you attack the tail, it will simply turn and bite you. You must strike the head. Klaus participated in the July plot against Hitler and was murdered by the SS in the final days of the war.

A Protestant Nazi *NS-Frauenschaft* leader in Cologne by the name of Auguste Henke narrowly escaped execution herself. After the invasion of Poland in September 1939 she wrote a letter to a friend in which she condemned Hitler for waging war and expressed her belief that she was not the only person who predicted that Germany would pay for its aggression. The letter was opened as part of a routine inspection and she was arrested and imprisoned. Her husband too was interrogated and strongly advised to divorce her if he wanted to distance himself from his wife's seditious remarks. Auguste was eventually released, presumably for fear that she might use her influence to promote her opinions, or the authorities might have made allowances for the work she had done for the Party.

Sophie Scholl

'Isn't it true that every honest German is ashamed of his government these days? Who among us has any concep-tion of the dimensions of shame that will befall us and our children when one day the veil has fallen from our eyes and the most horrible of crimes – crimes that infinitely outdistance every human measure – reach the light of day?'
(First Leaflet distributed by the White Rose)

While a few disgruntled citizens may have grumbled about the restrictions and demands imposed upon them, or heard of the persecution of the Jews and other enemies of the state with mute disapproval, it was left to a young girl, her brother and a small group of their friends to openly defy the dictatorship.

Sophie Scholl, the daughter of the mayor of Forchtenberg, had enthusiastically joined the BdM (League of German Girls) at the age of 12, but soon found she was out of step with her classmates. She had listened attentively as her father, brothers and even a few of her teachers discussed how Hitler was corrupting German youth and she had come to the conclusion that it was every Christian's duty to oppose the regime by any means possible. Her brothers and friends were arrested in 1937 for being members of the *Jugendschaft*, a non-political youth group, which confirmed her fear that the regime would stop at nothing to silence its critics, no matter how young and guiltless they might be. But it was after her father had been imprisoned for making a critical remark about Hitler in 1942 that she decided that the time for action had come.

Campaign of passive resistance

Sophie was by then studying biology and philosophy at the University of Munich, where her brother Hans was enrolled as a medical student. Together with a small circle of like-minded friends, including four other girls, they formed the anti-Nazi student organization known as the White Rose, to prick the conscience of those who remained impassive to the crimes perpetrated by Hitler's thugs. Their campaign of passive resistance was inspired by an anti-Nazi sermon given by Graf von Galen, the Bishop of Münster, in which he denounced the state-sponsored 'mercy killing' of the mentally and physically infirm and the administration's stated intention of usurping the authority and sanctity of the Church with its own neo-Pagan rituals. Bishop Galen's sermons and those of Cardinal Newman appealed to Sophie's humanity and Christian compassion, but it was her boyfriend's letters from the Eastern Front in May 1942 that convinced her that Hitler was destroying the soul of his own people.

Several male members of the group had been posted to the Russian Front for three months as part of a programme to acclimatize medical students to battle conditions, which only hardened their determination to oppose militarism on principle and fascism in particular. Willi Graf, a former member of the banned Catholic anti-Nazi 'Grey Order', witnessed the liquidation of the Lodz and Warsaw ghettoes and returned with first-hand accounts of SS atrocities.

Sophie's boyfriend, Fritz Hartnagel, wrote of having witnessed the execution of Soviet POWs and of the soul searching he subsequently suffered as he wrestled with his conscience. He had sworn an oath of unquestioning obedience to Adolf Hitler personally, which bound him to his commander-in-chief, but if those orders were immoral, was he obliged to carry them out?

While her boyfriend agonized over what action, if any, he should take, Sophie and her brother Hans recruited two close friends who shared their convictions, Willi Graf and Christoph Probst, and their mentor Professor Kurt Huber.

The men wrote six anti-Nazi leaflets which they left in public phone boxes and beer kellers, sending others through the mail to prominent academics and to sympathizers at other universities in Southern Germany. They also painted anti-Nazi slogans in public places, knowing that by doing so they were risking their lives and those of their families. Hans had discouraged his sister's involvement, but was persuaded that a girl would be less likely to be searched.

The sole survivor of the group, Jürgen Wittenstein, described how every member lived in a constant state of fear of being discovered, but they knew that if they failed to act they could not have lived with the knowledge that they had remained silent.

The government – or rather, the Party – controlled everything: the news media, arms, police, the armed forces, the judiciary system, communications, travel, all levels of education from kindergarten to universities, all cultural and religious institutions. Political indoctrination started at a very early age, and continued by means of the Hitler Youth with the ultimate goal of complete mind control. Children were exhorted in school to denounce even their own parents for derogatory remarks about Hitler or Nazi ideology. My own teenage cousin, for instance, threatened to denounce his father; and I was barely able to deter him by pointing out to him that he himself might end up destitute if his father were arrested and incarcerated.

In total, the White Rose published five of the six leaflets but on 18 February 1943 all were arrested while distributing the last of them in the grounds of Munich University.

The final sacrifice

During her imprisonment Sophie told her interrogators, 'I knew what I took upon myself and I was prepared to lose my life by so doing.'

The White Rose members were brought before the pitiless Nazi judge Roland Freisler, who was later to publicly humiliate the July 1944 plotters, and condemned to death. Just hours later they were beheaded. Other members of the group were rounded up, given peremptory hearings and executed. Of the original 12, only two survived. The widow of Kurt Huber received a bill for wear to the guillotine.

Their sixth unpublished leaflet was smuggled out of Germany, printed in England under the title *The Manifesto of the Students of Munich* and dropped in huge quantities by Allied aeroplanes in July 1943.

Sophie and Hans went to their deaths believing that their sacrifice would awaken other decent Germans to the horrors being performed in their name, but fear of the Gestapo ensured that they remained silent.

> The German people slumber on in their dull, stupid sleep and encourage these fascist criminals . . . through his apathetic behaviour he gives these evil men the opportunity to act as they do. (Second Leaflet)

CHAPTER EIGHT

The Gentle Sex?

A number of German women willingly participated in the Nazis' crimes against humanity

The Second World War, the most destructive conflict in human history, proved the old adage that war brings out the best and the worst in people.

More than 70 years after the fall of Hitler's evil empire, the eagerness with which 'ordinary' Germans participated in the wholesale murder of innocent civilians challenges our perceptions of human behaviour and reveals to what degree some personality types can be conditioned to carry out, or facilitate, inhuman acts while seeming to be indifferent to the suffering they inflict.

State-sanctioned cruelty

The capacity for human cruelty knows no national or racial boundaries, not even those determined by gender. In the wake of the German offensive to the East in 1941 more than half a million young women followed the victorious Wehrmacht and the SS death squads into Poland, Ukraine, Lithuania, Latvia, Estonia and Belarus, in their capacity as administrators, nurses, secretaries, guards, girlfriends and wives. They were transformed by what they witnessed, participated in and in some cases perpetrated, having been persuaded that they were racially superior to their victims.

In their case, ignorance and arrogance proved even more poisonous than the propaganda that had fed on those deficiencies. Thinking of the Slavs and the Jews as subhuman assuaged the women's guilt and relieved them of responsibility for their actions.

Women like Erna Petri, who shot Jewish children with her pistol at point-blank range on the estate she shared with her husband in Poland. When asked how she could murder them in cold blood when she had children of her own, she told her interrogators that they were not children, but Jews, and that she had wanted to demonstrate her worthiness to the men who worked for her. Such women were more numerous than historians have acknowledged and sadly they were not exceptional, but merely extreme manifestations of the homicidal automatons that Nazi indoctrination was designed to produce.

> **LIESEL WILHAUS SAW NOTHING WRONG IN ALLOWING HER THREE-YEAR-OLD SON TO WATCH HER SHOOT AT JEWS WORKING IN HER GARDEN**

In Poland in 1942 pregnant Vera Wohlauf stood in the market square of a small town wielding a horse whip, with which she helped her husband Julius round up the 11,000 Jewish inhabitants for transportation to Treblinka. Almost a thousand died, either shot, beaten to death or expiring from exhaustion in the fierce summer heat. Then there was Liesel Willhaus, the wife of an SS official, who saw nothing wrong in allowing her three-year-old son to watch her shoot at Jews working in her garden.

Women who killed children

In Ukraine, 22-year-old Johanna Altvater quickly tired of her administrative duties as secretary to regional commissar Wilhelm Westerheide and requested more involvement in the liquidation of the ghettos. Westerheide was more than happy to oblige her. Every additional man, or woman, made the round-up easier. Besides, it amused him to see Fräulein Hanna, as she was called, herding men, women and children into a truck like a cattle drover. And when she showed ruthless initiative in clearing a makeshift hospital single-handed it made him proud to see such dedication. Witnesses recalled how she strode into the room that served as a temporary children's ward, picked up the tiny occupants of each bed one by one and threw them screaming out of the window on to the pavement three floors below. Her bloodlust never sated, she would lure children with sweets then shoot them in the mouth with her pistol or grab them by the legs and smash their heads against a wall.

She threw the lifeless body of a toddler at his father's feet. 'Such sadism from a woman I have never seen,' the man remembered.

Gloating, 'Fräulein Hanna' then joined Westerheide and his men, who were eating and drinking at a long table in the open air as if at a fair. They were accompanied by music from a wireless or gramophone which was interrupted by gunfire and every so often one of the picnic party would leave the table and rejoin the massacre, to return a few moments later for more refreshments.

In Drohobych, Ukraine in June 1943 Josefine Block, the wife of the local Gestapo chief, carried a riding crop to lash prisoners waiting to be deported. When a little girl broke from the line and ran towards her crying for help, Brock reassured her, 'I will help you!', before grabbing the child by the hair, hitting her with her fists and knocking her to the ground, where she stamped on her head until she was dead. A certifiable psychopath, she would use her own pram to ram Jews in the street, killing at least one child, according to two witnesses.

Erna Petri, the 23-year-old wife of SS officer Horst Petri, was returning home from a shopping trip in Grzenda, Poland when she spotted six naked boys aged between six and twelve cowering in a ditch. Jews were routinely stripped naked for deportation so that they could be distinguished from the local Poles and Ukrainians. Frau Petri knew the children must have escaped from a transport taking them to an extermination camp near Lublin.

But being the mother of two children she invited them to her home, where she fed them and assured them that all would be well. Then she took them outside to a clearing in the woods behind her house and shot them in the back of the head.

Professor Wendy Lower, who collected countless eyewitness accounts of similar events, and confessions from previously unpublished records held by the East German authorities and other archives, concluded: 'The probability is that Petri could be multiplied a thousand times'.

Germanization of the East

Women were employed in an administrative capacity in almost every branch of the Nazi government and its military wings, including the SS. It was therefore only practical for them to join the Germanization programme when it moved east. They saw themselves like the pioneers in the Old West, or the British colonialists in Africa bringing civilization to the 'dark continent', whose natives were savage and expendable. The Jews would be eradicated, the Soviet commissars summarily executed and the partisans hunted down, then the indigenous population would be permitted to remain, provided of course that they agreed to submit to their masters.

It was as much a war of ideology as it was of conquest. There was no front line or battlefield, just one continuous frontier rolling ever eastwards, crushing communities that had existed for hundreds, if not thousands of years. The Nazis, those masters of double speak, or spin as we would name it now, called it the quest for *Lebensraum* ('living space'), the conquest and colonization of other lands, but it was a blueprint for ethnic cleansing long before that term was coined. Such an ambitious undertaking required a vast staff to document its plunder, both human and material, to ensure the distribution of fuel, food, ammunition and other supplies and to type, process and file the reports compiled by self-appointed racial experts.

The fascist state had legalized genocide and sanctioned brutality, persecution and intimidation, therefore murder and mistreatment of its enemies was not a crime. Quite the contrary. Refusal to participate would be viewed as dissent. Every citizen had the authority to enforce its racial laws with impunity. Showing mercy, or worse compassion, would be interpreted as disloyalty.

> **THE FASCIST STATE HAD LEGALIZED GENOCIDE AND SANCTIONED BRUTALITY THEREFORE MURDER AND MISTREATMENT OF ITS ENEMIES WAS NOT A CRIME**

In the Nazi mind, Eastern Europe was the breeding ground of Bolshevism and its inhabitants had spread the communist plague as they migrated west. It was every Aryan's duty to stamp out the vermin who disseminated it, be they male or female, adult or child. If the Führer had adjudged a specific group to be on a level with animals, then it was acceptable to treat them as such, to see them as a herd of cattle for slaughter as Franz Stangl, commandant of Sobibor and Treblinka, had described them, and not as individuals.

For the uneducated underclass who believed themselves to be undervalued and overlooked, the dictatorship offered the opportunity to wield power over those even lower in status than themselves. It was a typical tormenter–victim scenario and few of those with a latent capacity for cruelty could resist exploiting it.

For the remainder – the stenographers and shop girls, farm hands and village school teachers – it was a liberating experience to escape the repressive society in which they had grown up, and find themselves in a wide open land where the mere fact that they were German afforded them status and respect, even if that respect was born of fear. No more shortages, no constricting social conventions, no rules telling them how to behave. They were able to indulge in sex without commitment, drink and party when their work was done and spend their wages as they wished. An entire generation of 'nobodies' had become big shots overnight and, like the American hoodlums of the 1930s who similarly found themselves intoxicated by power without having earned it, they lost their heads. To put it mildly, they went more than a little mad.

As Holocaust historian Wendy Lower observed in *Hitler's Furies*, 30,000 women worked in an auxiliary capacity for the SS and the German police in Gestapo headquarters and prisons in the Eastern occupied territories, where 'psychological distancing was hardly an option and the likelihood of direct participation in mass murder was high'. A further 10,000 worked in the civil administration under Nazi *Gauleiters* (governors), as secretaries typing up the orders for mass executions and recording the details of organized atrocities as if they were documenting the production in a meat processing factory, while many more were there unofficially as the wives and girlfriends of the Nazi overseers. As Lower states, 'Some of the worst killers were in this group.'

Women such as Liselotte Meier, personal assistant to an SS officer who joined her boss in shooting parties in Belarus where the prey were human beings. She took an active interest in the executions and a perverse pleasure in deciding who should live and who should die. She spared the life of one woman only because the girl had been her hairdresser, while another secretary pulled a female prisoner from the condemned line because she hadn't finished knitting her overseer a jumper.

In the mind of the Nazi conquerors rounding up,

hunting down and executing their prey was hard work which required a reward in the form of food and other refreshments. So picnic tables would be set up by the women at the site of the deportations and in the killing fields as if it were a stag hunt or grouse shoot.

Not all of the victims were killed, imprisoned or enslaved. Thousands of children who were deemed to be ethnically German by virtue of their looks alone were torn from the arms of their mothers and fathers and transported to Germany. There they were adopted by state-approved surrogate mothers of sound Aryan stock who had miscarried or were infertile, to be raised as their own. Those children who did not accept their forced assimilation were abandoned to their fate in squalid children's homes that were little more than prisons, or in forced labour camps.

The Nazis, who had no reservations about killing babies and children, took 105 infants from the Czech village of Lidice after massacring their parents and sent them for Germanization in the Reich, even though they did not possess Aryan characteristics. It was an act of pure vindictiveness and was deemed a fitting punishment for harbouring the assassins who had killed Himmler's deputy, 'iron-hearted' Reinhard Heydrich. In all, 50–200,000 children are believed to have been stolen from the occupied territories in the East and the women who colluded in this appalling crime were never prosecuted.

Evil teachers

Wendy Lower unearthed many previously unpublished stories of collusion which ended tragically for both the innocent victims and their female persecutors. In the Bavarian village of Reicherbeuern, the elderly Friedrich K. recalled how a little girl in his class who suffered epileptic seizures had been excluded from school by her teacher because she considered the child a distraction. In any other country the child might have been admitted to a special school, or a regular school with a more tolerant teaching staff, but in Nazi Germany this particular teacher resorted to the euthanasia programme to rid herself of a troublesome child. Apparently the teacher took her own life later, presumably out of remorse at what she had done.

Evidently not all of the victims died violently at the hands of the Wehrmacht or the SS. Some went quietly to sleep and never woke up, the victims of 'ordinary' German women who had lost their humanity in a moment of madness. Even the educators who should have been nurturing young minds were collaborating with the regime, indoctrinating ethnic German children in the Hitler personality cult and its spurious racist pseudoscience. Two and a half thousand women worked as kindergarten and primary school teachers in one region of Poland alone. And when they fled back to Germany with the retreating army, they left the children behind.

Nurses who administered death

Nursing, by definition a caring and compassionate profession, was also corrupted by the Nazis, who used its young female members to administer lethal injections and supervise the gassing of the elderly, infirm and mentally disabled.

THOUSANDS SIMPLY MELTED INTO THE POPULATION, THEIR DEEDS ERASED WITH THE DESTRUCTION OF THE FILES BY THE VARIOUS INSTITUTIONS AT THE WAR'S END

Pauline Kneissler was one of the most notorious figures to be publicly named and prosecuted for her part in the euthanasia programme after the war, but there were thousands who simply melted into the population, their deeds erased with the destruction of the files burnt by the various institutions at the war's end and their surnames changed by the simple expedient of marriage.

Kneissler alone had to stand in

for the rest. She had toured mental institutions in Southern Germany, collecting up to 70 patients a day, every day for five years, to be brought to Grafeneck Castle where they were given 2cc of morphine-scopolamine before the gassing to render them docile. Kneissler admitted that they were not all serious cases and many were in 'good physical condition'. The fate of the patients was determined by two qualified physicians, who gave each a cursory examination before deciding who should die. She found the executions frightening at first, but she quickly became immune, reasoning, as did her colleagues, that 'gas doesn't hurt'. Perhaps the most extraordinary aspect of the nurses' involvement was that it was entirely voluntary and when informed that they could apply for exemption, none of the women in Kneissler's team did so.

An estimated 5,000 mentally disabled children were murdered in this way before Hitler ordered an end to the programme. Gerda Bernhardt's brother, Manfred, was among them.

Gerda remembered:

Manfred was a lovely boy, but he could only say 'Mama' and 'Papa' . . . He only learnt to walk very late too. He always liked to be busy. If my mother said, 'Bring some coal up from the cellar,' he wanted to do it over and over again. My father was in favour of putting him in some sort of children's hospital and then Aplerbeck came up as they had a big farm there and the boy might be kept occupied.

Aplerbeck was a 'Special Children's Unit', but none of the children would live to play on the farm.

They brought the boy into the waiting room. There was an orderly there when I was leaving. The boy stood at the window and I waved and waved and he waved too. That was the last time I saw him.

The bodies at Aplerbeck and Grafeneck and the other killing centres were cremated and the ashes shovelled into urns to be presented to the families with a certificate detailing the cause of death. But the official explanation was not always accepted. One family were notified that their loved one had died from an infected appendix, which the family knew to be false as the patient had their appendix removed ten years earlier. A catalogue of similar errors aroused the suspicions of grieving families who petitioned their priests to raise the matter with the authorities.

In September 1940 a Protestant clergyman, Pastor Braune, wrote to the Ministry of Justice condemning the conditions and treatment of his most vulnerable parishioners.

> Visits to the institutions in Saxony plainly show that the mortality rate is being increased by withholding food . . . Since the patients cannot possibly survive on that, they are made to take a drug (paraldehyde) which renders them apathetic. Oral and written reports make it movingly clear how the patients time and again call out 'hunger, hunger'. Employees and nurses who cannot bear this any more occasionally use their private means to still some of the hunger. But the result is beyond question. Hundreds have died a quick death in the last few months as a result of these measures.
>
> Nor are just those patients involved here who are absolutely beyond feeling. On the contrary, these are patients who know quite well what is happening and are watching how many funerals are taking place

each day. One report describes the mortal fear of a patient who had an exact presentiment of the fate that is to meet him and his fellow sufferers.

Hitler was forced to order an end to the programme of euthanasia in August 1941 after Bishop Galen of Münster had lodged an official protest with the District Attorney and the police.

> . . . lists are being made up in the hospitals and nursing homes of Westphalia of those patients who, as so-called 'unproductive citizens' are to be moved and soon thereafter killed . . . It probably is to protect the men, who with premeditation kill those poor, sick people, members of our families, that the patients selected for death are moved from near their homes to a distant institution. Some illness is then given as the cause of death. Since the body is cremated immediately, neither the family nor the criminal investigation department can discover whether there really was such an illness and what the cause of death was.
>
> I have been assured, however, that neither in the Ministry of the Interior nor in the Office of the Reich Leader of Physicians, Dr Conti, is there much effort to hide the fact that premeditated killings of large numbers of the mentally ill have already taken place and that more are planned for the future. [Source: *Kreuz und Hakenkreuz*, Neuhäusler]

But the murderous activities of fanatical Nazi midwives continued. They dutifully reported birth defects in unborn and newborn infants, which were considered sufficient grounds for compulsory abortion orders, euthanasia and the sterilization of the mothers.

Hitler's secretaries

'If you value and respect someone you don't really want to destroy the image of that person . . . you don't want to know, in fact, if disaster lies beyond the façade.'
(Traudl Junge)

For the average young girl working in a clerical job in Germany during the 1930s and 1940s life was routine and largely uneventful. But for Traudl Junge and her three female colleagues the events they witnessed at the 'Wolf's Lair' (Hitler's headquarters in East Prussia), in the Berghof and finally in the bunker under the Reichschancellery in Berlin became part of the historical record of the Third Reich and had a profound and lasting effect on each of them.

For Traudl, Christa Schroeder, Gerda Christian and Johanna Wolf were the secretaries of Adolf Hitler, and enjoyed a privileged position which brought them into closer proximity to the Führer than almost any other women in Germany. They were fascinated, in the truest sense of the word, by his personal magnetism and oblivious, or so they claimed, to the horrors which he ordered or authorized.

Traudl Junge

Junge later admitted to the journalist Gitta Sereny:

> It was more than charisma, you know. Sometimes when he went off somewhere without us, the moment he was gone, it was almost as if the air around us had become deficient. Some essential element was missing: electricity, even oxygen, an awareness of being alive – there was a . . . a vacuum.

She compared his absence to the silence that one suddenly becomes aware of when the electrical generator in a power plant is switched off and said that it was his will that energized everyone in his presence. To the four women, Hitler was a 'gentleman', a congenial and courteous employer. They could never imagine him being capable of the violent outbursts he was reputed to indulge in when anyone dared to defy him, or doubt the certainty of final victory. And as for the accusation that he had personally ordered the cold-blooded murder of millions of innocent civilians and the 'mercy killing' of countless severely physically and mentally disabled German citizens, they would insist it must all have been the work of Himmler or his subordinates acting on their own initiative. Junge went on:

> We never saw him as the statesman; we didn't attend any of his conferences. We were summoned only when he wanted to dictate and he was as considerate then as he was in private. And our office, both in the Reichschancellery and in the bunkers, was so far removed from his command quarters that we never saw or even heard any of his rages that we heard whispers about.

Junge claimed that their insular existence kept them blissfully ignorant of the impact the war was having at home and on the battlefield. And yet she lost her Waffen-SS officer husband in Normandy in August 1944, while significant events such as the surrender at Stalingrad in January 1943 had affected everyone in Hitler's headquarters.

> Then came that grey, rainy day when Fraulein Wolf, eyes red with weeping, met me on the way to the Führer bunker. 'Stalingrad has fallen. Our whole army has been annihilated. They are dead!' She was almost sobbing. And we both thought of all that

blood, and the dead men and the dreadful despair.

From that moment the role of the secretaries changed, the two young women and the two older women taking it in turn to provide their employer with company and innocuous conversation at meal times, with one on standby all through the night in case they were needed for dictation.

Junge continued:

> My colleagues told me that in the earlier years he talked incessantly, about the past and the future, but after Stalingrad, well, I don't remember many monologues. We all tried to distract him, with talk about films, or gossip, anything that would take his mind off the war. He loved gossip. That was part of that other side of him, which was basically the only one we saw.

Born Gertraud Humps in Munich on 16 March 1920, Traudl Junge was the youngest of the four secretaries when she was selected to work for Hitler in January 1943 and though she later expressed dismay at her own naïvety and wilful ignorance of the regime she served – albeit in a marginal capacity – she was not as simple-minded, nor as apolitical, as she made out.

Although exonerated by the de-Nazification court after the war, she was not, as she claimed, unaware of the nature of the regime she served or its policies towards those it considered 'undesirables' and enemies of the state. Her father, Max Humps, had been a member of the *Bund Oberland*, a *Freikorps* militia unit that had taken part in the Munich putsch, for which he and his friend Sepp Dietrich, the future leader of the *Leibstandarte* SS, Hitler's private bodyguard, were awarded the *Blutorden* (NSDAP Blood Order).

After her parents' separation, Traudl, her sister

and their mother moved in with their maternal grandfather. It was an intolerable situation for which the mother blamed Hitler, drilling into her daughters that the Nazis were not to be trusted and warning that they would turn children against their parents and have neighbours informing on anyone they suspected of not conforming.

Nevertheless, Junge became active in both the League of German Girls and the Faith and Beauty Society, which indoctrinated its female members in Nazi racist ideology. When father and daughter were reunited in 1936, after he had attained the rank of an officer in the SS, it seems highly improbable that their shared enthusiasm for National Socialism would not have been discussed.

Traudl wanted to be liked and desired a simple 'uncomplicated' life, so as soon as she was old enough to work she applied for a clerical post with the NSDAP, talking up her skills and a personal contact with Martin Bormann to secure a position in the Reichschancellery. Evidently she didn't see the point of harbouring a grudge if it meant losing the chance to work for the same organization that had encouraged her father to neglect his wife and children.

Traudl had been brought up by her mother, a general's daughter, to cultivate certain qualities which were to prove useful in her new post. She had been urged to be helpful, modest and circumspect and to make allowances for other people's idiosyncrasies. The perfect cipher, one could say, to serve a tyrant.

Traudl was no stranger to volatile and erratic behaviour. After her mother's schizophrenic brother came to stay, Traudl witnessed his periodic fits of paranoia with a mixture of amusement and alarm.

She learned to cultivate an attitude of indifference and detachment so as not to arouse his hostility. When he was forcibly sterilized she accepted it as a necessary precaution.

Junge had been just five when her parents separated and she later admitted that she found a substitute father figure in her future employer, Adolf Hitler. 'He was a pleasant boss and a fatherly friend. I deliberately ignored all the warning voices inside me and enjoyed the time by his side almost until the bitter end.' It was only decades later that she realized she had served 'the greatest criminal who had ever lived'.

At their initial meeting in the bunker at Rastenburg Hitler impressed Junge as 'a kindly old gentleman . . . speaking in a low voice and giving us a friendly smile.' Noticing that she was cold and nervous he offered to have a small electric heater brought in and reassured her that there was no need to be anxious as she could not possibly make as many mistakes as he had. This friendly and relaxed image contrasted with the stern military leader she had been accustomed to seeing in the newsreels.

It was only in the final days, she says, after Hitler had dictated his will and his political testament, that she realized she had been deceived and felt betrayed when he blamed the German people for their defeat.

> Our total collapse, the refugees, the suffering – of course I held Hitler responsible for that. His testament, his suicide, that was when I began to hate him. At the same time I felt great pity, even for him . . . He was a kindly paternal figure, he gave me a feeling of security, solicitude, for me, safety. I felt protected . . .

She compared it to being at the centre of an explosion where all is calm and claimed that her proximity to Hitler precluded any chance of gaining a real sense of the situation outside the bunker.

Of course, the terrible things I heard from the Nuremberg Trials, about the six million Jews and the people from other races who were killed, were facts that shocked me deeply. But I wasn't able to see the connection with my own past. I was satisfied that I wasn't personally to blame and that I hadn't known about those things. I wasn't aware of the extent. But one day I went past the memorial plaque which had been put up for Sophie Scholl in Franz Josef Strasse, and I saw that she was born the same year as me, and she was executed the same year I started working for Hitler. And at that moment I actually sensed that it was no excuse to be young, and that it would have been possible to find things out . . . We all knew about his hatred for the Jews, but I think nobody took it seriously enough . . . I think we were cowards . . .

Christa Schroeder

Christa Schroeder was a more formidable figure; a strongly opinionated woman who spoke bluntly and without fear of contradiction, at one point asking Hitler to his face if he still believed that the war could be won (an impertinence for which she was ostracized for several months). She was not as phlegmatic as Junge, being highly critical of anyone she considered insincere, and yet she would have us believe that she remained so close to Hitler that she had no inkling as to what he planned.

Born Emilie Christine Schroeder on 19 March 1908, like Junge she too was raised by an undemonstrative mother who showed her little affection. She claimed to have had no political convictions and that she would have gladly accepted employment with the KPD communist party in March 1930 if the opportunity had arisen. Instead, she applied for a secretarial post with the SA at their headquarters in Munich and was told that she had to join the Party in order to work there.

She became Hitler's personal secretary in 1933, working at the Reichschancellery until 1939, after which she accompanied him to the various command headquarters, remaining at his side until the bitter end.

Schroeder secured her first secretarial job with the NSDAP after replying to a small newspaper advertisement in a Munich newspaper. It was 1930, she was then just 22 and newly arrived in the city. She was told to report to the offices of the SA leadership (OSAF) at 50 Schellingstrasse, which had originally been the photographic studio owned by Heinrich Hoffmann. At the time Schroeder didn't know anything about the Nazi Party and was not familiar with the name of its leader, Adolf Hitler. She took the job because she needed it and considered herself fortunate to have beaten the other 87 candidates by virtue of her proven shorthand and typing skills as well as impeccable references.

Three years later she was transferred to the Radziwell Palace in Berlin, where Chancellor Hitler had installed himself and Eva Braun in adjoining apartments on the first floor.

'ONE DAY HITLER SAW US SITTING THERE AND ASKED IF HE MIGHT JOIN US. HE LATER CAME TO TEA ALMOST DAILY'

Opposite Hitler's office there was a long corridor off which were the rooms for his various aides. The first of these was the so-called Staircase Room where the stenographers waited through the long night hours in case they were called to take dictation. Frau Schroeder remembers:

One day Hitler happened to pass the Staircase Room at teatime, saw us sitting there and asked if he might join us. This hour of easy chatter was so much to his liking that he later came to tea almost daily. The Staircase Room was a place where he felt unburdened and I always had the impression that what he said there came from a secret memory box which at all other times he kept locked shut.

She recalled that he confessed to having played pranks on his school friends and that he also spoke of his parents and the beatings his father had given him.

> Before the dictation I would not exist for him, and I doubt whether he saw me as a person when I was at my typist's desk. A while would pass in silence. Then he would close in on the typewriter and begin to dictate calmly and with expansive gestures. Gradually, getting into his stride, he would speak faster. Without pause one sentence would then follow another while he strolled around the room.
>
> Occasionally he would halt, lost in thought, before Lenbach's portrait of Bismarck, gathering himself as it were before resuming his wandering. His face would become florid and the anger would shine in his eyes. He would stand rooted to the spot as though confronting the particular enemy he was imagining. It would certainly have been easier to have taken this dictation in shorthand but Hitler did not want this. Apparently he felt himself as if on wings when he heard the rhythmic chatter of the typewriter keys.

The typewriters were specially made for the Führer's secretaries, with 12mm characters so that he could read from the typed script without having to wear glasses in public.

> Her favourable impression of her 'chief' is the result of a highly selective memory, one which overlooked the implied threat he made when she asked how he would respond to a request to leave his employ – 'I would know how to prevent that.'

On another occasion Hitler revealed his lack of respect for his sisters, describing them as 'stupid geese' and going so far as to tell Angela's fiancé to break off their engagement because he considered her too stupid to make a good wife. His idea of the perfect housewife was Frau Kannenberg, the wife of his cook, who Schroeder described as 'well-groomed, circumspect and of quiet demeanour'.

In the company of his secretaries he would talk candidly of other women, admitting that his aristocratic patron Viktoria von Dirksen had introduced him to many influential figures in high society, but that in their company he had felt like 'an attraction in a zoo'.

Schroeder was shocked to discover that officers in Hitler's entourage were actively antagonistic toward his female staff and that what she had taken to be signs of friendship were merely the effects of alcohol. She spoke of hostility and deception emanating from this 'hollow society', which resented having women at its headquarters, and of having to listen to Hitler praise his secretaries when he felt that they merited his approval.

Johanna Wolf

Unlike her colleagues, Johanna Wolf took her memories of Hitler to the grave. She had been his longest-serving secretary, beginning in 1929, but she took her role as 'private' secretary literally and believed that if she had granted any interviews or accepted any of the lucrative offers she had received for her memoirs she would have betrayed a confidence to the man she had served. Hitler favoured her over the others and overlooked her shortcomings because she had been secretary to his old friend Dietrich Eckart, who had died in 1923.

But she was forced to answer questions as a witness in the pre-trial interrogations at Nuremberg in 1948, during which she told her interrogators that Hitler was 'the worst informed man in Europe'. She confessed to being 'amazed' at how little he knew, which she blamed on the fact that he rarely listened to anyone, unless they agreed with him. His supreme confidence in his own strategic 'genius' and his wilful disregard of the advice offered by his more cautious military advisers reaped rewards in the short term, but led to fatal errors and misjudgements that hastened the end of the war.

> I was more aware of the developments of the war than Hitler, and realized much sooner than he that the war was approaching its end . . . he had lost contact with people. Up to the very last day he still believed in victory.

The official document records that Frau Wolf believed Hitler knew of the atrocities in Poland and Ukraine because 'there had been considerable talk about this subject in the Reichschancellery', but that she thought it 'simply unimaginable' that he knew and tolerated what occurred in the concentration camps because in her experience 'he was always so kind'.

Angels of death

Some women volunteered to be Hitler's willing executioners. Of the 3,600 women who worked as guards and ancillary staff in the concentration and extermination camps, only 60 were brought to trial in the immediate post-war period (1945–49) and of these only 21 were executed.

In contrast, almost 5,000 men were prosecuted, of whom 500 were sentenced to death. The reluctance to indict German women for war crimes cannot be solely attributable to the Allies' deference to their sex, but rather to the fact that few committed murder with their own hands. Unlike their male colleagues, female guards were armed only with rubber or wooden truncheons with which they beat and brutalized the prisoners for any perceived infraction of the rules, such as stealing vegetables from the camp pigs who were fed more generously than the inmates. Only those who had deliberately set their dogs on defenceless female prisoners or beaten them to death could be indicted. Others escaped justice only because there were no surviving witnesses to testify against them. Lucie Adelsberger, a Jewish physician, described the scene in the women's hospital at Birkenau, where she worked under the supervision of the notorious Dr Mengele.

> The sick lie on straw sacks, all jumbled together, one on top of the other, and cannot stretch their sore limbs nor rest their backs. The beds bulge with filth and excrement, and the dead and the decomposing press with their stiffened bodies against the living who, confined as they are, cannot move away. Every illness in the camp is represented here: tuberculosis, diarrhoea, rashes induced by crawling vermin, hunger oedema where the wasted skeleton has filled itself with water to replace the vanished cell tissue, people with bloodshot weals caused by lashes of the whip, people with mangled limbs, frozen feet, wounds from the electric wire, or who have been shot at for trifles by a trigger-happy SS.

The very fact that the female guards lived among such scenes and did nothing to alleviate the suffering, but only intensified it for what a war crimes prosecutor called their 'malicious pleasure', was surely enough to condemn them.

Three of the worst offenders

Three of the worst offenders worked at Bergen-Belsen: Irma Grese, Elisabeth Volkenrath and Juana Bormann. Like the other female guards, they considered themselves to be members of the SS, although Himmler's elite would not accept women in their ranks. Officially they were members of the SS *Helferinnenkorps* (Women Helper Corps) or SS-*Gefolge* (retinue), a female support service which, unlike the regular SS, was not designated as a criminal organization after the war and therefore membership did not carry a mandatory prison sentence.

These largely poorly educated working class women had been recruited through newspaper adverts or plucked from the membership of the League of German Girls. However, Himmler made it known that he expected his men to treat them as comrades and the mere belief that they were serving in a legitimate branch of the SS gave them an exaggerated sense of their own importance and sanctioned their latent sadism.

Volkenrath was just 26 when the war ended, but she was already known as the most feared guard in the camp. She took sadistic delight in beating prisoners and training her dogs to tear them to pieces.

> **SHE STARVED HER DOGS SO THAT THEY WOULD BE RAVENOUSLY HUNGRY WHEN UNLEASHED ON A PRISONER**

Grese was 22 when she was hanged, earning her the dubious distinction of being the youngest woman to be executed under British jurisdiction in the 20th century. She carried a pistol and fired indiscriminately at prisoners she took a dislike to, referring to them as '*Dreck*' (dirt). She starved her dogs so that they would be ravenously hungry when unleashed on a prisoner and she would habitually beat prisoners to death, or whip them into submission, deriving a sadistic sexual satisfaction from seeing them suffer. In her defence she told the court, 'Himmler is responsible for all that has happened, but I suppose I have as much guilt as the others above me.'

Bormann, then 52 and prematurely ageing, was feared

for having trained her wolfhounds to attack prisoners and savage them to death. A religious zealot, she had abandoned missionary work to join the SS and thereafter directed her energies into tormenting her victims, having first weeded out those too old to work from the new arrivals and sent them to the gas chambers.

At her trial, her defence attorney described her as having a 'weak nature' that could not resist the urge to dominate those in her charge. She informed the court that she had only applied for the job to 'earn more money' and attempted to pass the blame on to another guard who she claimed resembled her and who also owned a dog, but the judges decided this elusive person was pure invention and found her guilty. Bormann did not appeal against the death sentence and seemed resigned to her fate. Prior to her execution all she could say was, 'I have my feelings.'

Purveyors of cruelty and death

The female guards had all been trained at Ravensbrück, which was the only camp exclusively for women. Sixteen SS personnel found themselves in the dock in December 1946, including five women – head nurse Elisabeth Marschall (61), *Aufseherin* (guard) Greta Bösel (39), *Oberaufseherin* (supervisor) Dorothea Binz (27) and *Kapos* (trustee prisoners) Carmen Mory and Vera Salvequart.

Marschall was charged with mistreating prisoners and assisting in inhuman experiments and Binz was found guilty of beating, whipping and shooting female prisoners. It was also believed that she had hacked another to death with an axe during a work detail. Bösel had been assigned to supervising the selection process as a 'work input overseer', which was a euphemism for choosing which of the new arrivals would be spared for slave labour and which would go straight to the gas chamber.

A further five women stood accused of murder at the third Ravensbrück trial in April 1948, for their part in the deaths and ill-treatment of young girls at the Uckermark satellite camp. Two were acquitted and two were sentenced to imprisonment, leaving SS *Oberaufseherin* Ruth Closius to mount the scaffold alone. She had been found guilty of torturing and murdering men, women and children.

At a seventh series of trials in July 1948 two more women were sentenced to death – 60-year-old Emma Zimmer and 36-year-old Ida Schreiber. Others received death sentences but these were subsequently commuted.

Ruth Neudeck, a guard at a Ravensbrück sub-camp was notorious for her cruelty. She had once slit the throat of a prisoner with the sharp blade of a shovel. For this and countless acts of vicious brutality she was sentenced to death.

Dr Herta Oberheuser was one of several female physicians who lent their skills to the service of Nazi pseudoscience, inflicting pain on her unwilling patients by injecting them with oil and evipan. She also rubbed foreign objects such as glass, wood and nails into open wounds to observe if they would heal without treatment. She appeared defiant and unrepentant in the dock during what became known as The Doctor's Trial in December 1946, the only woman among the 23 defendants. After hearing from 85 witnesses and reading 1,471 documents, seven of her co-defendants were sentenced to death, 9 were given lengthy prison sentences and 7 were acquitted. Herta was found guilty but escaped the death sentence, though her child victims would have no doubt demanded it had they lived. She received a 20 year-sentence but served less than half, after which she continued to work as a doctor until a former inmate recognized her and the authorities prohibited her from practising medicine.

Auschwitz's sub-camps and satellite camps
The name Auschwitz has become synonymous with genocide. But in addition to the main site which housed

the gas chambers where an estimated one million people died, there were two sub-camps and 40 satellite camps on the outskirts of Oświęcim, Poland, where unknown numbers died from typhus, starvation, beatings and as the result of sadistic experiments for which there was no scientific basis.

In the winter of 1947, 21 defendants were tried at Kracow for their part in the systematic extermination, starvation and ill-treatment of men, women and children, of which only two were women. Maria Mandel had been commandant of the women's camp and Therese Brandel a guard.

Mandel was said to be highly intelligent and a lover of classical music, which gave her the idea to organize a camp orchestra made up of inmates, who would play at roll call and at public executions. She was known for keeping Jews as 'pets', sending them to the gas chamber when she had tired of them, and was said to have been personally responsible for supervising the deaths of half a million prisoners.

Both were found guilty and sent to the gallows.

Alice Orlowski was also tried at Kracow. She had served at several camps, where she was feared for her habit of whipping prisoners across the eyes and for throwing children on top of groups of adults gathered together for the gas chambers, in what she called a 'space-saving operation'. Remarkably, she was spared the death sentence and given a life sentence of which she served only ten years. She died during a second trial.

Two more women from the SS detail at Auschwitz were arrested at a later date, tried and condemned to death. They were Elizabeth Lupka and Margot Drexler. A former inmate remembered Drexler:

Once Mrs Drechaler [Dreschler] came, with her huge bloodhound, undressed everybody, took away even our shoes, and we had to stand for hours completely naked, none of us were thinking of life any more, the gas chamber seemed unavoidable.

Hangman felt compassion

Five women who had served as guards at Stutthof concentration camp near Danzig were publicly hanged with their SS male comrades before a crowd of several thousand onlookers, after a trial conducted by the Poles. The women smiled and joked during the trial thinking that they might be acquitted because of their sex or given short prison sentences, but the charges were too grave to merit clemency. Wanda Klaff told the court, 'I am very intelligent and very devoted to my work in the camps. I struck at least two prisoners every day.'

Three more were executed for their crimes at other camps before the Allies' appetite for justice had been satisfied.

Else Ehrich had been the women's camp commandant at Majdanek concentration camp. She went to the gallows in October 1948 at Lubin in Poland. Ruth Hildner, a former guard at Zwodau, Flossenbürg in Czechoslovakia was executed in Czechoslovakia in May 1947 and Sydonia Bayer was tried and hanged in Poland.

> **THE BRITISH HANGMAN ALBERT PIERREPOINT FELT COMPASSION FOR SOME OF THE YOUNGER WOMEN**

The British hangman Albert Pierrepoint briefly felt compassion for some of the younger women, but was told by a soldier who had witnessed the liberation of the camps, 'If you had been in Belsen under this lot, you wouldn't be able to feel sorry for them.'

For some of the survivors even the death sentence was not enough to bring them a sense of justice. They had seen so many dead bodies and so many acts of unspeakable brutality that they were numb to the death of their oppressors.

One survivor, Kitty Hart, found satisfaction in taking the coat from a captured guard at Salzwedel. When asked by an American army officer why she was wearing it she told him, 'All that time when we were freezing, some of us to death, we hated those vicious bitches in their wind-proof, waterproof coats. And now I have one for myself.'

Sins of the mothers

It's always the innocents who suffer. But it wasn't only the Jews, Gypsies, Jehovah's Witnesses and other 'undesirables' who were murdered and brutalized by the sociopaths who served the Nazi state. The Nazis also slaughtered their own. The physically disabled and the mentally infirm were legally disposed of by lethal injection under the euthanasia programme by physicians and nurses who had taken an oath to preserve and respect all human life. Then there were the homosexuals who had been denounced by their fellow citizens as 'degenerate' and the political opponents who dared to question a regime which feared free speech more than the enemies beyond its borders.

There were others too. The forgotten victims of Hitler's tyranny were those who were irreparably damaged by merely living through the madness inflicted upon them by a psychotic system and traumatized as Germany was reduced to rubble.

Abandoned by her Nazi mother

Little Helga Schneider was just four years old when her mother abandoned her, her 18-month-old brother Peter and her husband to join the SS with whom she served as a concentration camp guard at Sachsenhausen, Ravensbrück and Auschwitz-Birkenau. When their father was transferred to another city, Helga and her brother went to live with their mean and spiteful stepmother, who beat and starved them so that they wouldn't grow up like their mother.

When the stepmother couldn't cope any longer with the little girl's disobedience, as she perceived it, she committed her to a mental institution ('a storehouse for unwanted children, for those who were considered unworthy of belonging to the Aryan race because they were blind, deaf-mute, crippled, paralysed, dwarfs, subnormal and so on.' [Source: Schneider, *The Bonfire of Berlin*]) where she was force-fed, subjected to a series of harrowing tests and confined in a windowless isolation cell in the basement for days at a time. Her stepmother only agreed to take her back when the staff determined that there was nothing wrong with the child.

When Helga was reunited with her brother she was horrified to see that he had been transformed from a cheerful child into a freakish automaton programmed to repeat banal Party slogans and chatter excitedly about being taken to see the Führer, as if Hitler was Father Christmas. He recited the names of Hitler's inner circle as another boy might learn the names of the players on his favourite football team and performed his party piece to please his stepmother, which consisted of memorized soundbites from Goebbels' speeches with suitably melo-dramatic gestures. It was a nightmare from which Helga knew she could never wake up.

Unable to accept her stepmother's strict discipline, Helga rebelled and was then taken to a 'boarding school' which was run by an anti-Nazi headmistress, who spoke frankly and at great risk to herself about the tyranny they were all living under and how 'horrible' the Führer was. He was a 'crazed megalomaniac' who was dragging Germany to disaster. He hated the Jews, black people, ballet dancers, poets and priests and had ordered the burning of books opposing National Socialism. He had taken the headmistress's widowed sister and her two three-year-old twins to a concentration camp just because she had married a Jew.

Living among the ruins of Berlin

The school offered Helga a real home, a sanctuary from the insanity that was raging just a few miles away in the capital. But the respite didn't last. She was taken back to the city by her stepmother, where she witnessed scenes that haunted her for the rest of her life. 'We are living like ghosts in a vast field of ruins. All power has been cut off, no gas, no electricity and even the water has to be scavenged. Phones can be heard ringing in bombed-out buildings, but no one is there to answer them. Personal hygiene is a luxury few can afford and hot meals are a fantasy to be dreamt about. There are rotting corpses in the streets and people joke that the living smell worse than the dead. We risk our lives to bury our excrement.'

The survivors were reduced to huddling in basements and ripping pages from books to use as toilet paper. Helga was distraught to see that Peter had become an emaciated haggard little boy and still he raved about the Führer and teased Helga that she wouldn't be taken to the Chancellery if she wasn't nice to him. After what she had heard about the Führer, Helga didn't want to go, but as their aunt worked in the Propaganda Ministry they were going to be treated to a personal tour of the bunker.

When the great moment came Helga was unimpressed.

Hitler shuffled towards the line of children like an old man, his head trembling, his left arm hanging limply by his side. She wondered, could this be the same man who once whipped vast crowds into a frenzy? He took the hand of each child in turn and asked a perfunctory question before passing on to the next, while a female orderly trotted behind him with a basket filled with bars of marzipan to mark the occasion.

Helga was next. Hitler held out his hand. It was hot and sweaty 'like that of a person with a fever'. She took it and looked into his eyes. He had a penetrating gaze that made her uneasy. They gleamed strangely, 'as though there is a goblin dancing inside them'. His face was grey, unlike the portraits hanging in the anterooms. He looked 'damaged'. A dense network of wrinkles around the eyes, the cheeks flabby, the features disintegrating.

He asked her name and if she liked being in the Chancellery bunker. She lied and said, 'Yes'. He withdrew his hand and she felt a great sense of relief. He handed out the marzipan and moved on. It was over.

Back in the tenement basement there was no chance of sleeping for more than an hour or two. Night and day the air raid sirens screamed, the ground shook, the walls trembled, masonry fell, crushing those sheltering underneath, and choking clouds of brick dust made the air unbreathable.

The interminable onslaught of the senses was broken only by long periods of eerie silence and anxiety. Rumours reached them that the Soviets had overrun the city. An SS soldier burst in, raised his Luger to his mouth and spattered his brains all over the wall. Then – inexplicably – there was nothing but silence. There were no more sirens. No flurry of earthquakes. Even the muted thump of artillery shells and the crackle of machine gun fire had stopped. But it was not the end. A new fear gripped Helga and the small band of survivors huddled in the airless cellar. The Ivans were coming. They would rape the women and steal what crumbs of food they had left.

Her mother was a sadistic killer

Everything comes to an end. Even Helga's ordeal. She survived and turned her back on the Germany of her wretched childhood. She moved to Italy and married. She had a son of her own, but she could not forget her mother and, in 1971, she answered a letter from Vienna asking if she would come to visit. Helga was prey to myriad emotions, but she was compelled to make the journey out of curiosity and the vain hope that her mother might have the decency to explain why she abandoned her children.

She met a stranger who looked strangely similar to herself. But there was a black hole between them: no hugs, no tearful reunion, reproaches and recriminations. Nothing. Just a perfunctory greeting and the sense of her mother's grim satisfaction that she had managed to induce her daughter to make the trip.

Traudi Schneider was a manipulative, emotionless woman who never had any feeling for her children. She didn't need any further desensitizing to condition her to treat her prisoners no better than cattle. But the *Harteausbildung* SS induction programme trained her and many like her to herd naked, terrified and starving women and children into the gas chambers and take a pride in her efficiency. When Helga finally plucked up the courage to visit the old woman she had never called 'mother', she was shocked to find herself face to face with a stranger who looked uncannily like herself but who expressed no regrets. 'I was condemned by the Nuremberg Court to six years' imprisonment as a war criminal, but none of that matters any more. With Nazism I was somebody. Afterwards I was nothing,' Schneider told her.

Traudi talked of working under infamous Auschwitz commandant Rudolf Hoess as if it was something to be proud of and was surprised that her daughter was not impressed. She also spoke candidly of the day she sent an acquaintance to die in a camp brothel as punishment for a perceived slight. The only time she showed a hint of genuine emotion was when she betrayed a sly smile when talking of sending infants to their death. She casually admitted that she had assisted the camp doctors in their sadistic experiments, bringing up gruesome details in expectation of approval and betraying disappointment when Helga couldn't hide her disgust. But even more chilling was the moment Traudi opened her wardrobe and brought out the uniform that had 'suited her terribly well' and which she had kept pristine for 30 years. 'Why don't you try it on?' she asked, with a barely suppressed hint of pride. 'I'd like to see it on you.'

Helga's life had been profoundly damaged. 'Had I forgiven my mother? Yes, I had forgiven her the hurt she had done to us, to her husband, to her children. But as for all the other things she was guilty of, only her victims had the right to forgive.'

Afterword

It is difficult to imagine how anyone living in Nazi Germany could remain callously indifferent to the crimes perpetrated by the dictatorship or how they could justify the torture, imprisonment and murder of thousands of their fellow citizens as mere 'excesses' committed by the more fanatical elements in Hitler's regime. But the unpalatable fact is that in the ten years from Hitler's appointment to the Chancellorship on 30 January 1933 until the shock defeat of the once invincible German Sixth Army at Stalingrad on 30 January 1943, life in the Reich was almost too good to be true for millions of 'ordinary' Germans.

After the privations that had followed Germany's defeat in 1918, there had been only the briefest respite before the Great Depression had wiped out savings, forced the closure of businesses, created mass unemployment and stimulated runaway inflation. This saw the price of essential foodstuffs increasing by the hour, until people were transporting millions of marks through the streets in wheelbarrows to buy a loaf of bread. So once the economy had been stabilized and there was work for all, it was natural for the grateful citizens to venerate Hitler as the saviour of the nation. He had restored their pride, fulfilled his promise to bring them bread and jobs and unified the nation. Even Franklin D. Roosevelt hadn't achieved that.

On the surface the Nazis cultivated a community spirit and promoted the return of traditional family values, with the Party supplanting the Church as the moral centre of society (although the Nazi leadership didn't always practise what they preached). The family unit was deemed to be sacred and a more simple, natural life was envisaged as desirable for both the rural and the urban population, with outdoor group activities being organized under the 'Strength Through Joy' programme and holidays away from the cities being offered to deserving workers and their families, albeit with a measure of National Socialist propaganda thrown in. Enrolment in youth groups was compulsory, but parents didn't generally object as it was viewed as part of the programme to produce healthy minds and healthy bodies. Only later did the Hitler Youth betray its true purpose – the training of boys for the armed forces.

After the seizure of Czechoslovakia in March 1939, there could be little doubt as to Hitler's intentions to conquer Europe, but no-one would dare criticize his audacious re-occupation of the Rhineland, the annexation of Austria or the seizure of the Sudetenland, which saw the return of millions of Germans into the greater Reich. And when war came it was not the bloody stalemate of the Great War as many had feared, but a blitzkrieg as German armour rolled over Poland and through Belgium, Luxembourg and Holland, bringing the 'old enemy', France, to her knees within weeks and sending the British scuttling back across the Channel to await the invasion. The Germans couldn't believe their luck; their faith in their Führer had been justified.

But all of this came at a price. The first German concentration camps were built in 1933 – beginning with Dachau as soon as Hitler became Chancellor – in order to neutralize political opponents, specifically the Social Democrats and Communists. Gradually other categories of 'undesirables' were rounded up: Jews, Jehovah's Witnesses, homosexuals, Gypsies and dissenting Catholics. The Gestapo had the power to arrest, interrogate and incarcerate anyone who was suspected of opposition to the regime. By the end of the war, an estimated 11 million Jews and 'enemies of the state' had died in Nazi concentration camps across Europe.

But did the ordinary women of Germany manage to insulate themselves from what was happening around them by buying into the lie that they had no part to play in 'politics', an untruth perpetuated by an administration that had conditioned them to believe that they were incapable of understanding such matters? Perhaps, but it is difficult to imagine that German women were not involved in politics when 13 million were active members of the Nazi Party.

Germany's women must have realized that their Jewish neighbours were gradually disappearing, along with other 'undesirables'. And it was difficult to claim to be unaware of the concentration camps; many political prisoners were reputedly released from Dachau before 1938 and they must have talked about their experiences there. Later on, when the number of deportations was too great to ignore, a wide cross-section of German society was actively participating in the 'resettlement' programme – railroad workers, clerks, secretaries, transport drivers, building workers, bankers, tax officials (who located Jewish property), etc.

Some said nothing because they lived in fear of the Gestapo, whose informers were everywhere; they were inclined to look the other way in order to save their own skins. Several studies of female denunciation in the Third Reich have been made, among them Helga Schubert's *Judasfrauen* (Aufbau-Verlag, 1990), which suggests that a relatively large number of women denounced the people around them for a variety of reasons, from jealousy to petty vindictiveness, such as the neighbour who denounced two women she suspected of living together as a lesbian couple.

Hausfraus apart, around 500,000 female nurses, teachers, secretaries, clerks, wives and girlfriends went east into the occupied territories. Almost all of them were volunteers and fully aware of the atrocities that were being committed, because their duties were intimately linked to the genocide. Some perpetrated horrors in their own right. Within Germany, the nurses who took part in the euthanasia programme were given the opportunity to move on to other duties, but most of them chose to stay where they were.

On the other hand, many women bravely resisted the Nazis and others helped Jewish families, risking imprisonment and the loss of their own children. Some caring attendants did what they could to combat hunger in the institutions where they worked. But whatever the circumstances, it is difficult to view the majority of German women as passive or unseeing observers.

Apart from those women who followed the dictates of their consciences, irrespective of any danger to themselves, a question mark hangs over the role of many German women during the war. Claudia Koonz's observation that German women were involved in 'preserving the illusion of love in an environment of hatred' is what many would have had the world believe when the war came to an end. They saw no reason to feel guilt or shame, they said, because they hadn't committed a crime. They had obeyed the law and if that law was an immoral one, then it wasn't for them to question it. Had they not been expressly forbidden from taking an active role in affairs of state?

Whatever atrocities had been committed were surely no worse than those the western democracies had practised themselves. After all, concentration camps had been introduced by the British in the Boer War, America had legalized racial segregation, practised enforced sterilization in some states and engaged in genetic engineering. The Allies had committed atrocities against civilians when they bombed Dresden and other German cities. Some even insisted that the Holocaust was a fiction – it was Allied propaganda, an exaggeration. They turned away from the mounds of rotting, emaciated corpses in the newsreel footage of the liberation of Belsen and shook their heads in disbelief when the charges were read out at Nuremberg. It was all a lie. De-Nazification could never hope to rid them of this distorted perception. The fact was that they had been a part of something so unspeakably awful they could only survive by denying that it had happened at all.

'Every man is guilty of all the good he failed to do.' (Voltaire)

Bibliography

Bruns, Jana F. *Nazi Cinema's New Women* (Cambridge: Cambridge University Press, 2009)

d'Almeida, Fabrice *High Society in the Third Reich*, trans. Steven Rendall (Cambridge: Polity Press, 2008)

Fromm, Bella *Blood and Banquets* (London: G. Bles, 1943)

Guenther, Irene *Nazi Chic?: Fashioning Women in the Third Reich* (Oxford, New York: Berg, 2004)

Junge, Traudl *Until the Final Hour: Hitler's Last Secretary* (New York: Arcade, 2004)

Knopp, Guido *Hitler's Women* (New York: Routledge, 2001)

Koonz, Claudia *Mothers in the Fatherland: Women, the Family and Nazi Politics* (New York: St Martin's Press, 1988)

Kubizek, August *The Young Hitler I Knew* (London: Greenhill Books, 2006)

Langer, Walter 'Interview with Dr Bloch 5 March, 1943' in *Hitler Source Book* (Office of Strategic Services, 2002)

Ratcliff, J.D. 'My Patient Hitler' by Dr E. Bloch, *Collier's* magazine, 15 March, 1941

Roland, Paul *The Illustrated History of the Nazis* (London: Arcturus, 2009)

Roland, Paul *The Nazi Files* (London: Arcturus, 2014)

Stoltzfus, Nathan *Resistance of the Heart: Intermarriage and the Rosenstrasse Protest in Nazi Germany* (New Brunswick, NJ: Rutgers University Press, 2001)

Resources

www.accounts.greyfalcon.us/junge.html

www.aforcemorepowerful.org

www.alphahistory.com/nazigermany/women-in-nazi-germany

www.brightlightsfilm.com/46/nazi.php#.UuDpE_tFCt9
www.en.wikipedia.org/wiki/Nazism_and_cinema
www.en.wikipedia.org/wiki/Women_in_Nazi_Germany
www.express.co.uk/expressyourself/232762/Fashion-houses-
    that-dressed-the-Nazis
www.fold3.com/page/285925288_the_women_hitler_loved/
www.fsmitha.com/review/r-meisner.htm
www.henrymakow.com/hitlersfirstmurderhtml.html
www.history.ac.uk/reviews/review/1233
www.historytoday.com/blog/2013/03/fashion-and-third-reich
www.hsse.nie.edu.sg/staff/blackburn/NazipropagandaFACT.
    html
www.janethynne.com/the-nazi-wives/
www.jewishvirtuallibrary.org/jsource/Holocaust/women.html
www.newstatesman.com/society/2008/07/nazi-uniforms-black-
    fashion
www.nizkor.org/ftp.cgi/people/h/hitler.adolf/ftp.cgi?people/h/
    hitler.adolf//oss-papers/text/oss-sb-koehler
www.otto5.com/_archive/Interview_Part_1.htm
www.spartacus.schoolnet.co.uk/GERraubal.htm
www.spiegel.de
www.studentpulse.com/articles/206/hitlers-use-of-film-in-
    germany-leading-up-to-and-during-world-war-ii
www.jewishpress.com
www.usmbooks.com/carinhall_story.html

Blind Spot: Hitler's Secretary (2002) is a feature-length
    documentary released by Sony Pictures Classics
'Secretary to Hitler' is a 23-minute extra episode of the
    documentary series *The World at War* (1974)

Index